MEADE

MILITARY PROFILES
SERIES EDITOR
Dennis E. Showalter, Ph.D.
Colorado College

Instructive summaries for general and expert readers alike, volumes in the Military Profiles series are essential treatments of significant and popular military figures drawn from world history, ancient times through the present.

MEADE

Victor of Gettysburg

Richard A. Sauers

BRASSEY'S, INC.
Washington, D.C.

Cataloging in Publication Division
101 Independence Ave., S.E.
Washington, D.C. 20540-4320

Library of Congress Cataloging-in-Publication Data

Sauers, Richard Allen.
    Meade : victor of Gettysburg / Richard A. Sauers.—1st ed.
        p. cm.— (Military profiles)
    Includes bibliographical references and index.
        ISBN 1-57488-418-2 (alk. paper)—ISBN 1-57488-749-1 (pbk. : alk. paper)
    1. Meade, George Gordon, 1815–1872.   2. Generals—United States—Biography.   3. United States. Army—Biography.   4. Meade, George Gordon, 1815–1872—Military leadership.   5. United States. Army of the Potomac.   6. Gettysburg, Battle of, Gettysburg, Pa., 1863.   7. United States—History—Civil War, 1861–1865—Campaigns.   I. Title.   II. Series.

    E467.1.M38S28 2003
    973.7'349'092—dc22   2003021612

Hardcover ISBN 1-57488-418-2
Softcover ISBN 1-57488-749-1
(alk. paper)

Brassey's, Inc.
22841 Quicksilver Drive
Dulles, Virginia 20166

FIRST EDITION

10 9 8 7 6 5 4 3 2 1

Contents

Maps

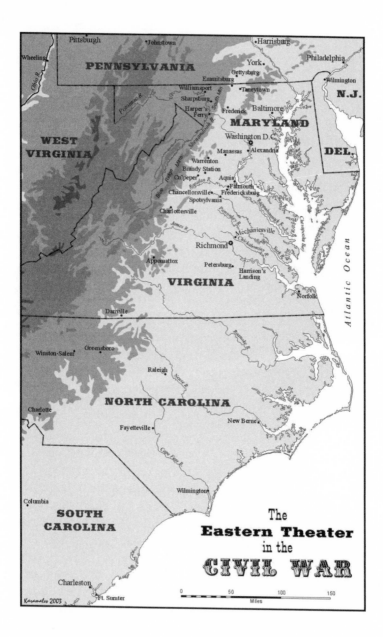

The Eastern Theater in the Civil War

Preface

Nearly every student of the American Civil War knows the name George Gordon Meade. As the victor at Gettysburg, his name has been linked with that famous battle ever since July 1863. But because Meade failed to pursue and destroy Robert E. Lee and the Army of Northern Virginia after Gettysburg, Meade's reputation suffered at the time. The Army of the Potomac had no shortage of politicking and backbiting generals, who cast barbs at Meade by saying that the battle of Gettysburg was a Federal victory in spite of Meade's generalship. Operations in the fall of 1863 did little to aid Meade's reputation.

In 1864, Lt. Gen. Ulysses S. Grant decided to accompany the Army of the Potomac in its campaign against Lee's troops. Because of this, Meade, even though he retained command of the army until the end of the war, was thrust into the background as Grant received most of the favorable press coverage. Meade was not even present at Appomattox when Lee signed the surrender terms in April 1865.

Meade himself presented a controversial picture even to his contemporaries. Brig. Gen. Alexander S. Webb, Meade's last chief of staff, wrote sometime after the war that "I never knew of a man who could make so many personal enemies through his 'righteous dealing' with unworthy generals as did Genl. George Gordon Meade." Webb understood Meade perfectly. The general was truthful to a fault, and at times needed to keep his opinions of others to himself rather than risk either making enemies or having his words misconstrued. But Meade also made long and lasting friendships with several other generals as well as with most of his staff officers.

Meade was famous throughout the army for his volatile temper, and those on whom it fell would later leave uncomplimentary portraits of the general. Meade's nephew Richard Bache reasoned that Meade's temper was no better or worse than that of other generals. Lt. Col. Theodore Lyman, one of the general's volunteer staff officers, thought that Meade's reputation for a quick temper when things did not go right forced others to ensure that they did things correctly so that the general would not lose his temper at them.

Because of Meade's personality, peers often viewed him differently. Assistant Secretary of War Charles A. Dana wrote many unflattering descriptions of the general, as did some of Grant's staff officers who thought that Meade should have been replaced as army commander in 1864. Generals such as Phil Sheridan and Baldy Smith penned outright lies in their memoirs in order to grab more glory for themselves at Meade's expense. Horace Porter, who served on Grant's staff in 1864, wrote the following description of Meade:

> General Meade was a most accomplished officer. He had been thoroughly educated in his profession, and had a complete knowledge of both the science and the art of war in all its branches. He was well read, possessed of a vast amount of interesting information, had cultivated his mind as a linguist, and spoke French with fluency. When foreign officers visited the front they were invariably charmed by their interviews with the commander of the Army of the Potomac. He was a disciplinarian to the point of severity, was entirely subordinate to his superiors, and no one was more prompt than he to obey orders to the letter. In his intercourse with his officers the bluntness of the soldier was always conspicuous, and he never took pains to smooth any one's ruffled feelings.[1]

The major nemesis in Meade's life was Maj. Gen. Daniel E. Sickles, the political general in command of the Army of the Potomac's Third Corps. Sickles disobeyed orders at Gettysburg, marching his corps off of Cemetery Ridge to a salient position at the Peach Orchard, where his corps suffered heavy losses on July 2. Sickles himself was wounded and incapacitated for further active service. Meade generously wrote in his official report that Sickles had simply misinterpreted his orders, but Sickles, ever the politician, would not stand for this interpretation of his actions and began spreading falsehoods about Meade's generalship at Gettysburg. The Joint Congressional Committee on the Conduct of the War used Sickles and other disgruntled generals to blacken Meade's reputation. Although Meade survived this harassment, the resulting mass of vituperative literature has cluttered the history of Gettysburg and resulted in a lack of appreciation for Meade's performance in that great battle.

Meade himself never wrote a memoir. Disgusted with Sheridan's press coverage during the Appomattox Campaign, Meade wrote to this wife that "I don't believe the truth will ever be known, and I have a great contempt for History."[2] He died in 1872, within two months of turning fifty-seven. Overshadowed by more famous generals such as Grant and William T. Sherman, Meade has never received his due. He has been the subject of only three full-length biographies. Historians are divided over his wartime performance and thus the reader will find a wide range of interpretations of Meade's character and generalship.

This biography contains the salient features of General Meade's life. Throughout this book, I have corrected previous historical inaccuracies and provided some new interpretations of Meade's career. All such interpretations are my own. Readers interested in learning more about Meade will find relevant material in the Bibliographic Note at the end of this volume. Perhaps this new biography will spur fresh research about one of the Civil War's most famous and most misunderstood generals. If so, then I have succeeded in my intentions.

Chronology

1856–61   Duty with Great Lakes survey.

1857   Promoted to captain.

1861   Promoted to brigadier general of volunteers on August 31. Assigned to Pennsylvania Reserves division as commander of Second Brigade.

1862   Saw action at Gaines's Mill (June 27) and Glendale (June 28), where he was wounded. Returned in time to lead his brigade at Second Manassas (August 29–30). Commanded Pennsylvania Reserves at South Mountain (September 14) and Antietam (September 17), where he was in temporary command of the First Corps. Promoted to major general of volunteers on November 29. Led division at Fredericksburg (December 13). Placed in command of the Fifth Corps on December 23.

1863   Led Fifth Corps in Chancellorsville Campaign (April 27–May 5). Placed in command of the Army of the Potomac on June 28. Led the army at Gettysburg (July 1–3), Bristoe Station, and Mine Run. Promoted to brigadier general in the Regular Army on July 3.

1864   Led the army during the entire year, fighting at The Wilderness, Spotsylvania, North Anna, Cold Harbor, and Petersburg. Promoted to major general in the Regular Army on August 18.

1865   Led the army at Petersburg and in the Appomattox Campaign. Assigned to the command of the Military Division of the Atlantic.

1866   Conducted operations along the Canadian border against Fenian raids. In August, placed in command of the Department of the East.

1867   Appointed to command of the Third Military District.

1868   Appointed to command of the Department of the South.

1869   Reassigned to command of the Military Division of the Atlantic.

1872   Died from pneumonia on November 6. Funeral took place on November 11, with burial at Laurel Hill Cemetery in Philadelphia.

MEADE

Chapter 1

The Antebellum Years

GEORGE GORDON MEADE, the victor of Gettysburg, was born on December 31, 1815, in Cádiz, Spain. He was the eighth child and second son of Richard Worsham Meade (1778–1828) and Margaret Coats Butler. Margaret hailed from Perth Amboy, New Jersey, while Richard Meade was from a prominent merchant family of Philadelphia. Richard had entered his father's business and rose through the ranks to eventually manage the family merchant transactions in Spain, hence George's foreign birth.

At the time of Richard Meade's sojourn in Spain, that country had been invaded by Napoléon and was wracked by war. Meade wholeheartedly supported the loyalist cause and placed his vast fortune in the hands of the crown. After the French were driven out, Meade expected to be repaid, but was instead thrown into prison for two years in an effort to silence his mounting criticism of the government. Mrs. Meade, who had returned to America, actively sought her husband's release. Although influential men such as Congressman John Sergeant, who brought

Meade's plight before Congress, tried to help the family, the government stalled.

Before anything could be done, word of Andrew Jackson's invasion of Spanish-held Florida reached both capitals and relations quickly deteriorated. Meade was released from prison in 1818 and came home two years later. The 1819 treaty between America and Spain threw the payment of any outstanding claims into American courts, and until his untimely death at age fifty in 1828, Meade continued to press his claim. His family never received any money.

The Meades at first remained in Philadelphia. Richard's son, George, at age eight, was sent to a private boarding school and remained there for three years. Then, the elder Meade relocated to Georgetown in order to better present his claims to the government. George was placed in the American Classical and Military Lyceum, a private boarding school in Mount Airy, near Germantown, just north of Philadelphia. This school was modeled on West Point and provided the young Meade with a solid educational foundation. While attending school there, George showed a particular aptitude for mathematics; he was also commended by the instructors as being a youth of promise for a bright career.

His father's death in late June 1828 ended Meade's stay at the lyceum. The family was suddenly much poorer and George's mother could not afford the school any longer. George then went to two boarding schools in Washington and Baltimore before his mother decided to apply for his admission to West Point. Young Meade had not shown any interest in the military, but West Point had an excellent reputation and his mother believed that upon graduation, he could resign and enter any profession he wished.

After an initial rejection, George Meade was admitted to West Point in the summer of 1831. He entered the academy that September as part of a class of ninety-four young men. During his four years at West Point, Meade exhibited his usual capacity for acquiring knowledge but also showed a dislike for routine military matters such as guard mount and drill. In July 1835, Meade stood nineteenth in a class of fifty-six and was breveted a second lieutenant in the Third Artillery. His classmates included George W. Morell, Montgomery Blair, Herman Haupt, Henry M. Naglee, Marsena Patrick, and Benjamin S. Roberts.

Immediately upon graduation, Meade spent the summer working as an assistant surveyor on the Long Island Railroad, then reported to his regiment in Florida. Lieutenant Meade was only in Florida a short time when he became wracked with fever because of his somewhat frail constitution. He was reassigned in the spring of 1836 to escort a party of Seminoles to the Indian Territory west of the Mississippi.

After completion of this task, Meade reported to the adjutant general in Washington. Following a short delay, he was assigned to duty at the Watertown Arsenal in New York. On October 26, 1836, Meade resigned his commission in favor of work as a civil engineer. From November 1836 through April 1837, his brother-in-law, Maj. James D. Graham, employed him as assistant engineer in the construction of the Alabama, Florida, and Georgia Railroad. Meade then received work surveying the mouth of the Sabine River. He next went to work on another military project, surveying the Mississippi River delta, which began in November 1837 and lasted about six months. Meade then journeyed to New York City and worked on the final report for the project, which occupied his attention until February 1839.

Meade then accepted the position of assistant engineer for the astronomical section of the border survey between Texas and the United States, a project that lasted through the first eight months of 1840. In August, Meade was appointed by the Secretary of War as civil assistant for the survey of the northeastern boundary line between the United States and Canada, which was under the direction of Major Graham.

Meade's mother continued to reside in Washington, and on his frequent visits there, Meade began courting Margaret Sergeant, the eldest daughter of Congressman John Sergeant, who had tried to help the Meade family in years past. After some initial opposition, the congressman gave his consent for Meade to marry his daughter. The happy event took place on December 31, 1840, at the Philadelphia home of the Sergeants.

Meade continued to work on the boundary survey, but as more and more rumors swirled about retrenchment on the Army's part—which would include not hiring civilians—Meade finally decided to reenter the Army. Thanks to Congressman Henry A. Wise of Virginia, who had also married one of Sergeant's daughters, Meade was appointed a second lieutenant in the Topographical Engineers on May 19, 1842, and was continued on duty with the boundary survey.

In November 1843, Lieutenant Meade was relieved from survey duty and ordered to report to Maj. Hartman Bache, who had headquarters in Philadelphia and was in charge of the construction of lighthouses and surveying the Delaware Bay. This position gave Meade the opportunity to remain at home while working nearby. His duties included the design and construction of a new lighthouse for the Brandywine Shoal in Delaware Bay, using the latest screw-pile technology from England.

By early 1845, the Meades had three children. John Sergeant Meade had been born on November 4, 1841. A second son, christened George, was born on November 2, 1843, and the couple's first daughter, Margaret, was born on February 26, 1845.

And then, on August 12, 1845, Lieutenant Meade unexpectedly received orders to report to Gen. Zachary Taylor at Aransas Bay, Texas. A boundary dispute with Mexico was heading toward open war, and Taylor's small force was expected to patrol the border and be prepared if the negotiations failed to be resolved peacefully.

Going by way of Washington, Cincinnati, and New Orleans, Lieutenant Meade reported to General Taylor in mid-September 1845. Capt. T. J. Cram was the senior topographical engineer, followed in seniority by Meade, then Lt. Thomas J. Wood. The unhealthy climate prostrated many officers and men with fever, and often Meade found himself the only engineer officer on duty. Finally, Meade came down with jaundice and was hospitalized. The chief surgeon urged him to go home to recuperate, but with both Cram and Wood gone, Meade felt that he had to remain on duty. The Army did not give its officers money to go home on leave, which for him would probably be a two-month stay at home. Lieutenant Meade reasoned that the Army would not assure him of another post once he recuperated. "At night," wrote the lonely Meade, "when I thought of seeing you and my dear children, the happiness I should enjoy in once more having you all around me, I would be almost crazy, and determined the next morning I would go and get my leave."[1]

But Meade stayed on duty with Taylor's army. Following Mexico's rejection of payment for a boundary drawn along the Rio Grande, Taylor was instructed to advance to the river in a show of force. To Meade fell the duty of plotting the line of march, which began in early March 1846. Watched by cautious Mexican patrols the entire time, the advance guard reached the river on March 29. Mexicans in ambush attacked but were repelled after seizing a couple of men as prisoners. Taylor's army settled into camp opposite the Mexican town of Matamoros. Meade, working with newly arrived engineer Lt. J. E. Blake, laid out the camp and regularly rode out to survey the terrain. He was accompanied by a strong escort owing to the prowling Mexicans who ambushed at every opportunity.

After a month of inactivity, Taylor took most of his army to Point Isabel to receive a wagon train of supplies and also to lure the Mexicans into a fight. While marching back to camp, Taylor's 2,200 men were confronted by about three times that number of Mexicans, led by Gen. Mariano Arista. The two forces clashed at Palo Alto on May 8. During this brief engagement, Meade acted as a messenger to subalterns along the line. Although horses were shot within yards of the lieutenant, he emerged unscathed from his baptism of fire.

The next day, May 9, the Mexicans came again to confront the Americans. The resulting battle of Resaca de la Palma resulted in a complete rout of Arista's forces. Taylor's men captured seven cannon, the enemy's pack train, their ammunition, and all their baggage. One general and several other officers were among the 150 prisoners. The proud Meade wrote a letter home on a piece of General Arista's stationery. Meade also was able to report that Lieutenant Blake accidentally shot himself and died, leaving the Philadelphian as the only topographical engineer with Taylor.

Taylor decided to cross the Rio Grande and occupy Matamoros. To that end, Meade was kept busy surveying the river and selecting a crossing place. After swimmers brought across boats from the opposite shore and planking was brought up from Point Isabel, the army crossed the Rio Grande on May 18 and occupied Matamoros without opposition. Taylor's army remained in Matamoros throughout most of the summer as volunteer regiments began to augment the Regulars. Meade was aghast at the unsoldierly discipline and lax camp sanitation of the volunteers. His letters home to Margaret were filled with denunciations of them and their decidedly unmilitary ways. The lieutenant also spent time surveying the countryside and wrote lengthy descriptions to his wife.

By mid-August, Taylor had moved his army a hundred miles up the Rio Grande to the small town of Camargo, the head of navigation of the river. Capt. W. G. Williams had joined the army as senior topographical engineer, and Meade remained a second lieutenant, even as others were promoted for their actions in the May fighting. Meade, as always publicly modest, voiced the opinion to his wife that his own role in the battles was minimal; he had done his duty and that was that.

From Camargo, Taylor directed his army toward the sizeable city of Monterrey, at the foot of the Sierra Madre. By mid-September, Taylor's 6,000-man army was poised to strike at the fortified city. On September 19, Taylor rode out to reconnoiter the fortifications to the north of the city. The enemy opened with artillery and a cannonball passed within two feet of Lieutenant Meade before the party withdrew to select a camp. Meade and other officers spent the rest of the day surveying the enemy positions and drawing maps. After listening without comment to their report, Taylor decided to split his force and assail the city from both sides.

Lieutenant Meade was assigned to go with Gen. William Worth's Second Division, which marched around the city to its eastern fringe and attacked two hills topped by supporting fortifications. Meade and Worth dodged cannonballs as they surveyed the enemy positions. Worth's soldiers, after lying in a cold rain through the night, attacked on the morning of September 21. After wading through the cold Santa Catalina River, Worth's men scaled Federation Hill as the enemy fled; only twenty-three men had been lost thus far. Taylor's main attack had not made much progress, so Worth was ordered to go ahead and take the enemy position on Independence Hill.

It was raining again in the hours before dawn on September 22 when Lieutenant Meade helped guide the storming party up the steep slopes of Independence Hill. The men literally crawled forward, each man touching the one in front, careful not to kick loose stones or strike their rifles against the rocks. By dawn, the forward elements were in position and charged, only to find that most of the opposition had fled.

Taylor's two columns assaulted Monterrey the next morning, September 23, engaging in heavy fighting as the storming columns inched their way toward the central plaza. September 24 saw an armistice take effect. Taylor and the Mexican generals worked out an agreement by which the Mexicans evacuated the city and continued the armistice for eight weeks. Taylor had suffered 450 casualties and found he was fighting more than 9,000 Mexicans. Far from his base, he allowed the enemy to withdraw rather than risk further losses. To Meade, Taylor's decision made sense and saved the volunteers from being further disorganized and crippled. "[A]ny one who for four days and nights is in constant state of exposure to fire-arms of all descriptions will be very well satisfied to terminate so disagreeable an occupation," penned a relieved Meade to his wife.[2]

Meade and two comrades (Lt. John Pope and Lt. Jeremiah Scarritt) found an abandoned mansion in Monterrey and lived as well as they could for some time. Meade went out on occasional scouting expeditions, but Taylor's army lay inactive for several months. Taylor, a Whig, was not a favorite in Washington. The Polk administration sent Gen. Winfield Scott with a new army to attack Mexico from the coast. Taylor was instructed to send Scott all his Regulars and half of his volunteers, while he himself would remain with a smaller force to guard the American gains in northern Mexico.

Lieutenant Meade, with many regrets, accompanied the march of Taylor's troops to the port town of Tampico, where General Scott arrived in February 1847. The famous general decided to attack the port city of Veracruz, capture it, and use it as a base of operations against Mexico City itself. Accordingly, the army landed near the city on March 9. Meade, now reporting to Maj. William Turnbull, stood idly by as the Topographical Engineers were thrust into the background as other engineer officers with the army were given the most important duties. Meade complained to General Worth that his presence was ignored. Worth in turn asked Scott about Meade's role in the campaign, and when Major Turnbull retorted that he had more than enough engineer officers, Meade was ordered to report to engineer headquarters in Washington.

After a three-week journey, Lieutenant Meade arrived in Washington and was instructed to return to his duties under Major Bache. Meade visited his mother and took care of the monetary affairs of some deceased officers, then went home to a joyous reunion with his family. Appreciative citizens of Philadelphia presented the lieutenant with a handsome sword. Major Bache heartily welcomed Meade back and set him to work on the yet uncompleted Brandywine lighthouse. The major also sent Meade south that fall to the Florida coasts to survey possible sites for lighthouses.

Meade continued with lighthouse work until October 1849, when he received orders to report to Gen. David Twiggs in

Florida. Brewing trouble with the remaining Seminole Indians necessitated the construction of army outposts connected by roads. Twiggs assigned Meade this task and the lieutenant set to work, at first accompanied only by another soldier and a mule. Meade remained on duty in Florida until Twiggs considered the work done in February 1850. Meade then hurried home to Philadelphia, where his son Spencer had been born on January 19.

Meade continued to work on the Brandywine lighthouse, then returned to Florida to begin work on a lighthouse on Carysfort Reef near Key Largo. Meade was on duty there when he was promoted to first lieutenant in August 1851. In August 1852, the Topographical Engineers established the United States Lighthouse Board. Meade was appointed engineer for the Seventh District (Florida). He located five new lighthouses and supervised their construction. In the summer of 1853, Lieutenant Meade was sent to the Crystal Palace Exposition in New York to set up an engineering exhibit that explained to inquiring visitors the Fresnel lamp, which was used to throw a lighthouse beam across vast distances.

Meade then continued his arduous work on Florida lighthouses, eventually becoming the Seventh District superintendent. When Major Bache was transferred to the West Coast, Meade also assumed the supervision of the Fourth District (New Jersey and Delaware). Meade's duties sometimes allowed him to be home to assist his growing family (daughter Sarah was born in 1851 and daughter Henrietta in 1853, followed by son William in March 1855).

In 1856, Meade was transferred from coastal duty and sent to Detroit to assist with the ongoing survey of the Great Lakes, which had begun in 1841 and was yet uncompleted. The following spring, Meade was promoted to captain and placed in charge of the survey. The process entailed the mapping of the lake shores and navigation hazards, the charting of the lake bottoms to locate hidden dangers, and the mapping of projected ship channels. The duty also included the improvement of existing harbors as well as searching for potential sites that could be made into harbors. Sites for lighthouses, beacons, and buoys also had to be located.

After successfully fighting reduced budgets from Congress, Meade was able to hire more staff and procure additional equipment so that the survey of Lake Huron was completed and work was begun on Lakes Superior and Michigan. In 1858, Meade himself made an important change to the way longitude was determined, thus allowing for a more accurate reading than previously possible. Meade also worked on a number of technical details to assist the junior officers under his command. Indeed, Meade would later write that he considered his work on coastal lighthouses and the lakes survey as among the most important duties of his career.

But North and South were on a collision course as the 1850s waned, and Meade could see that cantankerous politicians in both sections were agitating the people of the United States. Meade wholeheartedly believed in the preservation of the Union and hoped that the radicals on both sides would calm down and return to a reasoned state of mind. Thus, in the 1860 presidential election, Meade voted for the candidacy of John Bell and Edward Everett, who represented the new Constitutional Union Party, a compromise attempt to sway conservative voters who opposed both the Republicans and Democrats.

But the Democratic Party split into Northern and Southern factions. Abraham Lincoln, with only 40 percent of the popular vote, won enough electoral votes to win the presidency. The ascendancy of the Republicans enraged the more radical politicians in the South, who feared that the Republicans would legislate an end to slavery. As a result, South Carolina seceded from the Union in December. By the time Lincoln was sworn in as the nation's sixteenth president on March 4, 1861, more states had left the Union to form the Confederate States of America, with former Secretary of War Jefferson Davis as president. Negotiations over federal property in the seceded states brought the divided nation to the verge of conflict. Controversy swirled around Union possession of Fort Sumter, which dominated the harbor of Charleston, South Carolina. Lincoln decided to maintain the fort and sent a relief expedition with more men and supplies. As a result, Confederate batteries opened fire on the morning of April 12, touching off the Civil War.

Chapter 2

The Pennsylvania Reserves

Following the Union surrender of Fort Sumter, President Lincoln asked the Northern states to supply 75,000 three-month militia to suppress the rebellion. Captain Meade and his subordinates were then in Detroit and were caught up in the frenzy that followed the opening of hostilities. On April 20, city officials demanded that all Federal officers with their commands be assembled in the city and publicly take the oath of allegiance to the government. Meade, imbued with the sense of duty prevalent in the Regular Army, convened his five junior officers and decided to boycott the mass meeting. The officers agreed that they did not need to take an oath of allegiance because they had already done so when they enlisted in the Army years before. Meade wrote later to a friend that "duty required that I should disregard all political questions and obey orders."[1] This point of view enraged several politicians, most notably Michigan Senator Zachariah Chandler. Meade's choice would later come back to haunt him in the spring of 1864.

Meade watched as his subordinates slipped away. Two of them—Robert F. Beckham and William P. Smith—resigned and left to join the Southern Confederacy. The others all received promotions and went off to join new units then being raised. Meade himself queried the War Department about a transfer to active duty. The captain borrowed money to send his family back to Philadelphia in the expectation that he would soon be ordered to a different command.

But as the days flew by into summer, Meade remained in Detroit, champing at the bit. He went to Washington in late June to petition in person for increased rank in one of the new Regular Army regiments. Meade was promised that something would be done for him, but he returned to Detroit empty-handed. Professor Joseph Henry, secretary of the Smithsonian Institution and a member of the Lighthouse Board, visited Mrs. Meade in Philadelphia and sought her help in convincing her husband to remain in charge of the Great Lakes survey. Professor Henry realized that Meade had a scientific mind and had a brilliant future that might be derailed if he went on active military duty.

But Mrs. Meade wanted to see her husband receive a commission in the volunteer forces then being raised across the North. Captain Meade first heard a report that he would be assigned to the command of a company of Topographical Engineers in the new army that Maj. Gen. George B. McClellan was assembling in Washington. Governor Austin Blair of Michigan offered Meade a commission as a colonel of one of the new Michigan regiments then being raised.

Unexpectedly, in early September, Meade received word that he had been commissioned a brigadier general of volunteers, to rank from August 31. Perhaps Mrs. Meade had a hand in working behind the scenes to ensure her husband's promotion. Pennsylvania Senator David Wilmot's name cropped up in correspondence about Meade's promotion, as did state Attorney General William M. Meredith and Governor Andrew G. Curtin. General Meade received orders to report to General McClellan for assignment to duty. Meade turned over the lakes survey to his old instructor, Col. James D. Graham, and hastened eastward.

Once he arrived in Washington he reported to McClellan, commander of the Army of the Potomac, which was the principal Federal army in the eastern United States at the time. Meade was instructed to report to Brig. Gen. George A. McCall, who commanded the division known as the Pennsylvania Reserves, a splendid force of thirteen infantry regiments and attached artillery and cavalry. McCall appointed Meade to the command of the Second Brigade, composed of the Third, Fourth, Seventh, and Eleventh Pennsylvania Reserves, a total of about four thousand soldiers. Brig. Gen. John F. Reynolds led the First Brigade, and Brig. Gen. Edward O. C. Ord was in charge of McCall's Third Brigade. In total, McCall's division included more than twelve thousand eager young men in blue.

Meade quickly immersed himself in the new details of a commander of troops. He wrote to Margaret that his duties thus far were "principally paper work. You would be astonished to see the amount of writing and papering required of a general in the field. . . . Nevertheless, being regulations, one has to comply with the requirements, however foolish they may seem."[2] The general also purchased a horse named Old Baldy, who had been wounded at the first battle of Manassas, also called Bull Run, and was owned by two other officers before Meade obtained him. Old Baldy quickly became Meade's favorite horse, but one that would aggravate the general's staff because his gait was faster than a walk and not quite a run, making it hard for other horses to keep up with him.

When Meade joined the division, its camp lay at Tenallytown, northwest of the capital, in Maryland. In early October, the reserves marched into Virginia and occupied a new camp, christened Pierpont after the loyal governor of Virginia. Throughout the winter, the reserves drilled, performed guard and picket duty, and occasionally sent expeditions out into the surrounding countryside to obtain supplies and watch for Confederates.

Other than the occasional foraging expedition, there was little to do but drilling to make the volunteers into better-trained soldiers. Meade was worried about his men. "They do not any of them, officers or men," Meade wrote to his wife, "seem to have the least idea of the solemn duty they have imposed upon themselves in becoming soldiers." That his men were brave Meade had no doubt, but he opined that none of the volunteers were aware that they might be killed in an unexpected battle with the enemy. Meade could say of himself that he was there from his own sense of duty, calmly awaiting the test, and that folks could say of him that he did his duty.[3]

Ord's brigade defeated a Confederate foraging expedition at Dranesville, Virginia, on December 20, winning the Army of the Potomac's first victory. Meade's brigade was on alert, but remained in camp and saw no action. At this time, Meade wrote that he was beginning to realize that the men he commanded were good soldier material, but, owing to the elective system by which the officers were chosen, he also was in command of a number of bad officers, men who were "ignorant, inefficient, and worthless."[4]

The general was able to obtain a ten-day leave of absence in mid-January, giving him the chance to go home for a visit. The family generally was doing well, although his eldest son, Sergeant, was troubled by a tubercular cough. Son George had been accepted at West Point but was struggling and piling up demerits. Meade returned to his brigade, which remained in camp, waiting for the roads to dry and the spring campaign to begin.

As winter came on and McClellan's army remained in its camps around the capital, politicians began to snipe at the general, and Meade agonized over his superior's flogging by the press and civilians who knew nothing about the Army. Although Meade was elated about the Union successes in February 1862, he suggested to Margaret that there should be no boasting about triumph over the South. The war was far from decided, Meade thought, and the South was not a foreign foe. Meade believed that the North should act more like a parent who is compelled to chastise an erring child and does so with a sad heart.

In March, President Lincoln, over McClellan's objections, divided the Army into corps. McCall's division was assigned to the First Corps, led by Maj. Gen. Irvin McDowell, who had suffered the defeat at Bull Run in July 1861. Movement finally occurred shortly thereafter, as the Confederates abandoned their forward positions around Manassas Junction and withdrew to the south. McClellan's advancing troops found empty fortifications; McCall's men advanced as far as Hunter's Mills, a trek of only fifteen miles. The Army of the Potomac then returned to Alexandria and began embarking on ships for the voyage to the Virginia Peninsula. McClellan planned a quick march up the Peninsula to Richmond, the Confederate capital.

At the last minute, worried over the safety of the capital, the administration detached McDowell's troops and ordered the First Corps to remain in position to ensure the safety of Washington. McCall's division eventually marched south to Manassas, then began inching down the Orange & Alexandria Railroad. McDowell's command was renamed the Department of the Rappahannock, which suggested to Meade that the troops would move south to cooperate with McClellan's advance up the peninsula. On April 29, Meade's brigade reached Falmouth, a small village across the Rappahannock from Fredericksburg. The brigade had repaired several miles of the railroad, and Meade was glad to finally receive orders to proceed to the front.

The division went into camp to await further orders. On May 4, Ord was promoted to major general and given command of a new division that was added to McDowell's command. He was replaced by Brig. Gen. Truman Seymour as commander of McCall's Third Brigade. McDowell's three divisions were then poised to march south to threaten Richmond from the north, but the strategic offensive by Stonewall Jackson in the Shenandoah Valley upset Federal plans. McDowell's corps was held back but on June 9 the administration ordered McDowell to detach McCall's Pennsylvania Reserves to join McClellan, who was clamoring for more men, thinking he was outnumbered by the Confederates.

McClellan had landed the 120,000-man strong Army of the Potomac at Fort Monroe in late March, then moved up to confront the Confederate entrenchments across the peninsula at Yorktown. Overestimating the enemy strength, McClellan initiated siege warfare rather than attack. The main Confederate army withdrew from Manassas to reinforce Yorktown. Gen. Joseph E. Johnston, the Southern army commander, evacuated the Yorktown defenses on May 3 and began a withdrawal toward Richmond. After a sharp battle at Williamsburg on May 5, McClellan's army closed to within a dozen or so miles of the Confederate capital by late May. Taking advantage of the flooded Chickahominy River, which divided McClellan's divisions, Johnston attacked on May 31 at Seven Pines, but was rebuffed after two days of fighting. Johnston was wounded during this battle and replaced by Gen. Robert E. Lee. McClellan, still believing he was outnumbered, kept badgering the administration for more troops. Thus, McCall moved to join the Army of the Potomac.

Chapter 3

Meade's Brigade in Combat

O N JUNE 11, 1862, Reynolds and Meade were sent downriver about six miles below Fredericksburg, where a fleet of transports awaited the troops. Reynolds and Meade got their men aboard the ships, but before Meade and his staff could board their assigned ship, McCall and his officers crowded aboard, leaving a fuming Meade ashore to await either new ships or the return of those already loaded. Meade quickly composed an irate letter detailing all of this to Margaret, but then reopened the letter and wrote a postscript at 5:00 P.M. to say that more ships had arrived. After supervising the loading of his brigade wagons and ambulances, the general was finally off to rejoin his regiments.

The Pennsylvania Reserves were taken by water down the Potomac River, up the York River, then up the Pamunkey River to White House Landing, the main Union supply base. General Meade arrived at the landing on the morning of June 14 to find the occupants of the landing agog at the prospect of the enemy. General J. E. B. Stuart's Confederate horsemen had begun their ride around the Union army and had attacked Tunstall's Station on the York River Railroad. Meade's brigade baggage train, protected only by a company of the Fourth Reserves, had escaped capture when the guards put on a brave front and scared the enemy away. Meade caught up with his brigade near the Chickahominy River and assumed command.

The division remained in camp until June 17, when it marched up the river to New Bridge. On the nineteenth, McCall received orders to post his regiments in the vicinity of Mechanicsville, on the extreme right of the Army of the Potomac and only five miles from Richmond. His division was assigned to the Fifth Corps, Brig. Gen. Fitz John Porter commanding. McCall left Meade's brigade in camp at New Bridge to guard the river from that point to his advanced position near Mechanicsville. Still worried about how his men would perform in battle, Meade conveyed to Margaret the story of how groups of them would foolishly expose themselves as spectators during an occasional artillery duel, as the artillerists of both sides fired at each other's working parties. Meade berated the men for their disobedience of orders to remain hidden, then let the camp be shelled for some time to show his soldiers what war was really like. He then had the camp moved to a more secure location.

General Lee, commanding the Army of Northern Virginia, decided to attack Porter's corps, the only Union force north of the Chickahominy. The attack was scheduled to begin on June 26, when Gen. Stonewall Jackson's corps, arriving from the Shenandoah Valley, would threaten the Union position at Mechanicsville from the northwest as Confederate Maj. Gen. A. P. Hill's division crossed the Chickahominy and attacked McCall's men as well.

When Jackson's advance was delayed, Hill crossed anyway and launched a frontal attack against the Reserves, solidly positioned behind Beaver Dam Creek. Seymour's brigade was on the left, with Reynolds on the right. McCall ordered Meade to bring up his brigade and act as a reserve. Leaving the Eleventh Reserves to maintain the picket line along the river, Meade hurried forward with the Third, Fourth, and Seventh Reserves. Both the

Third and Seventh regiments went into line to support the hard-pressed front line, but the Union artillery broke up all the Confederate attacks, which were further disorganized by the accurate rifle fire of the blue-clad infantry. By the end of the day, Hill had suffered at least 1,400 casualties, as opposed to only 361 from McCall's division.

Just before dawn on June 27, McCall received orders to withdraw. Porter was aware of Jackson's advancing corps and decided to place his men in a strong position behind Boatswain's Swamp, located six miles to the rear. McCall's division formed behind the main line as a reserve. The Confederate army followed the retreating Unionists and began a series of assaults at 2:30 that afternoon, resulting in the battle of Gaines's Mill. Porter's three divisions, assisted by fresh troops near the close of the battle, managed to hold together long enough to withdraw from the field after dark. Heavy pressure from the enemy attacks led to the use of McCall's regiments on a piecemeal basis, reinforcing parts of the line threatened by enemy attacks.

Meade's four regiments thus went into battle at different times and places on the field. As a result, Meade could only ride from place to place, rally any faltering units he saw, and encourage his men. By seven o'clock that evening Jackson's corps was on the field and the heavy Confederate attacks finally cracked Porter's line. Regiment after regiment began to retreat toward the Chickahominy bridges, covered by fresh troops arriving to stem the enemy advance. Meade's Eleventh Reserves, together with the Fourth New Jersey, were surrounded and captured in the heavy musketry smoke. General Reynolds was cut off and tried to hide in a swamp, but was discovered the next morning and captured. McCall's division also lost nine of its cannon from three different batteries. All told, the division suffered 1,651 casualties.

Following the defeat at Gaines's Mill, Porter's corps reformed south of the Chickahominy as McClellan began to change his base to Harrison's Landing on the James River. During the initial part of the Union withdrawal, McCall's troops escorted the army's Artillery Reserve through White Oak Swamp to Quaker Road. After accomplishing this task, on June 29 the division was instructed to follow the rest of the corps toward the James. Porter was supposed to retire via Quaker Road, but a local guide led the corps on a smaller old road also known as Quaker Road. Meade's brigade was in the advance and the general soon suspected that they were on the wrong road. After he informed McCall of his suspicions, McCall halted the column and so informed Porter, who instructed the Reserves to bivouac by the side of the road even as the rest of the corps countermarched in an effort to locate the proper road.

And then, Porter seems to have forgotten about McCall, who, lacking any orders for several hours, drew up his men in formation parallel to Willis Church Road, the main avenue of retreat for the Army of the Potomac. General McClellan came on the scene and ordered McCall to hold his position until the army's baggage trains had passed his rear. McCall deployed his men with Seymour on the left, Col. Senaca G. Simmons's brigade (Reynolds's) in the center, and Meade's on the right. Meade's left flank was on Long Bridge Road. Batteries E & G, First United States, Lt. Alanson M. Randol commanding, was unlimbered to the right of the road on Meade's front, which, together with the rest of the line, was deployed in front of a belt of trees and faced a large open expanse of fields with more trees beyond.

Worried about the woods to his front, General Meade, accompanied by Seymour, rode forward to discover that a squadron of the Fourth Pennsylvania Cavalry was the only force between the reserves and enemy pickets, evidently covering a larger force of the Confederates. After McCall learned the situation, he sent forward the First and Third Reserves as skirmishers to cover his front line. To McCall's right was Brig. Gen. Phil Kearny's division of the Third Corps, with Gen. Joseph Hooker's division of the same corps located some 600 yards south of Seymour's left.

This was the situation when Gen. James Longstreet's fine division of six brigades advanced to the attack sometime around

5:00 P.M. Longstreet was followed by A. P. Hill's large division. Lee hoped to send these two divisions against the center of the retreating Union army in an attempt to break the retreating column before it reached the James River.

The resulting fighting, known variously as Glendale, New Market Crossroads, Frayser's Farm, and Charles City Crossroads, was a nightmare for the outnumbered Federals. The Southern attacks began on the Union left and gradually extended along the entire line of McCall's division. Meade, after detaching the Third Reserves as pickets, only had available the Fourth and Seventh Reserves, plus the remnant of the Eleventh. The general used these units to protect Randol's six cannon. Two regiments of Brig. Gen. Cadmus Wilcox's Alabama Brigade charged Randol's position, and after being twice repelled, managed to reach the battery on their third attempt. Aided by the Fourth Reserves, Randol's gunners engaged the enemy in a vicious hand-to-hand combat, finally driving the Alabamians back. A later attack by a Virginia brigade of Hill's division captured Randol's guns and drove the remnant of Meade's brigade back into the woods to the rear.

At some point during this fighting, Meade was wounded when a bullet hit him in the upper right side and ranged down, exiting from his back just above the hip. After giving instructions to Lieutenant Randol to continue the fight but save his guns if he could, Meade rode a short distance to the rear, where he discovered that his other mount, Blacky, had also been wounded. The general at first supposed that his right arm, which had also been hit, was the more serious wound, but he became faint from loss of blood and had to be assisted to the rear.

Dr. Isaac Stocker, the division's chief surgeon, encountered Meade as the general was going to the rear. Stocker, also wounded, accompanied Meade to the division hospital, which was now crowded and too near the front line to be safe if the Union army continued to retreat. By a stroke of good luck, Meade's personal two-wheeled headquarters cart was found hurrying along the road, flagged down, and the general and Dr.

Stocker climbed in to continue their journey to the rear. Meade, unsure of the future, unbuckled his Mexican War sword and belt and entrusted it to one of his surviving orderlies. This unnamed orderly evidently "lost" the sword soon after. It was retrieved by a Virginia soldier, in whose family it remained until after Meade's death, when it was returned to his family.

Sometime after midnight, the cart with Meade and Stocker arrived at Haxall's Landing on the James. Here, Brig. Gen. Seth Williams, adjutant general of the Army of the Potomac, met the general and vacated his own tent in order to make the wounded Meade as comfortable as possible. Later that day, Meade wrote a brief letter to his wife advising her of his wound, which, according to Dr. Stocker, was not serious but required constant medical attention. The general alerted his wife that he would be coming home by boat. This hospital ship docked in Baltimore on July 3, where Margaret met her wounded husband. Unable to travel by rail, Meade was transferred to another ship, which proceeded to Philadelphia. The general arrived at his Pine Street home on Independence Day. There, the family physician, Dr. Addinell Hewson, was waiting to examine and redress Meade's painful wound. The doctor found that the bullet had entered his body at an acute angle, but missed any vital organs when it was deflected by a rib, passing out Meade's back an inch or so to the right of his spine.

Meade was forced to remain inactive while his wound slowly healed. A few days after arriving home, he was surprised to see his servant, John Marley, appear at his house with both horses (Blacky and Old Baldy) and personal baggage. Marley had heard that the general had died of his wound, so he had managed to recover the horses and returned to deliver them to the family. Impatient at being away from his duty, Meade chafed as he read the war news in the local newspapers. Maj. Gen. John Pope was now in command of a new Army of Virginia, while McClellan's Army of the Potomac remained on the peninsula, although it seemed that some of McClellan's troops would reinforce Pope.

Nine days before his leave was due to expire, General Meade

left Philadelphia, en route for Harrison's Landing. He reached the Pennsylvania Reserves' camp to find out that the division was embarking on ships bound for Aquia Creek. Meade learned that both McCall and Reynolds had been exchanged, that Mc-Call had been ordered to Washington, and that Reynolds was in command of the division. Meade reported to Reynolds the next morning, who advised his friend that he would continue in brigade command once the division was reassembled near Fredericksburg. So advised, Meade took the mail steamer to Baltimore and then found transportation to Aquia Creek, arriving there on August 17. Once in camp, Meade visited his old brigade, "and was much gratified by their turning out by companies and cheering me. I stopped at each company and said a few words, indicating my gratification at being once more among them, and commending them for their good conduct in battle." Meade was well pleased at his warm reception and was able to gauge that his men were sincere in their desire to greet their trusted general again.[1]

Reynolds assumed command of the division on August 21. During the ensuing reorganization, Meade received command of the First Brigade, which consisted of the Third, Fourth, Seventh, Eighth, and Thirteenth Reserves. Seymour received the Second Brigade, and newly promoted Gen. C. Feger Jackson the Third Brigade. The division went into camp across the Rappahannock from Fredericksburg. On August 22, orders came to pack up and join Pope's army, located farther to the northwest along the Rappahannock. The reserves took up the line of march sometime after ten o'clock that night, with Meade's regiments in advance. The night was dark and stormy, wrote Meade, and the troops lost their way. By morning, they had managed to cover only four miles. On August 23, "one of the hottest days I almost ever experienced," according to Meade, the division marched twenty-three miles to come within supporting distance of Pope's troops.[2] The division reached Rappahannock Station in time to discover that Pope was falling back toward Washington, responding to Confederate units under Stonewall Jackson that had gotten in his rear and destroyed his main supply base at Manassas Junction.

Pope misused his cavalry and instead sent his infantry divisions trudging north to locate Jackson before Longstreet's corps could unite with him. If Pope managed to isolate Jackson and attack with overwhelming strength, he would be able to destroy Lee's divided army. But Pope's luck did not hold out. Reynolds's division was attached to McDowell's First Corps, and led that corps as it marched along the Warrenton Turnpike toward the old Bull Run battlefield. Late on the morning of August 28, as Meade's brigade trudged along behind McDowell and his retinue, some of Jackson's artillerists fired a few shots at the distant Yankees; one shell exploded in the midst of the Eighth Reserves.

Meade quickly brought his regiments to a halt and deployed in line of battle, facing the direction of the enemy artillery. Battery C, Fifth United States, unlimbered, but its smoothbore Napoleons could not reach the enemy. Meade thereupon brought up Capt. James H. Cooper's Battery B, First Pennsylvania. Cooper's ten-pound Parrotts found the range quickly and the Confederates withdrew just as quickly. Meanwhile, Meade sent forward the Bucktails (Thirteenth Reserves) in skirmish order and the enemy backed off after less than an hour of desultory shooting. By one o'clock, Reynolds ordered Meade to withdraw his men and resume the march. Jackson, toward evening, finally decided to attack in strength once he learned that Longstreet was on the way. His attack fell on Gen. Rufus King's division of McDowell's corps, leading to the savage fighting on the Brawner Farm fields.

The Second Battle of Manassas opened the next day as Pope brought his troops to face Jackson's position in an unfinished railroad bed north of the old battlefield. Throughout the day, Jackson managed to repel several uncoordinated Yankee assaults. Reynolds's division spent the day on the Union left. Meade brought his brigade forward to the crest of a small ridge overlooking Groveton, unlimbered Cooper's battery, and deployed his infantry in support. Reynolds withdrew Meade later in the day after realizing that his line was unsupported by any other Union troops. Meade's skirmishers also noticed a buildup of enemy troops in their front. This was the arrival of Longstreet's corps, which went into position at right angles to Jackson's line, prepared to both defend Jackson's right flank and attack Pope's left.

The battle continued on August 30. Pope's attacks were repelled and Longstreet launched a massive flank attack that afternoon. His troops rolled up Pope's troops and precipitated a general withdrawal toward Washington. Reynolds deployed his troops on the Henry House Hill in an effort to slow down the victorious Confederates and allow the beaten Union army to retreat in safety. Meade's regiments occupied a portion of the Manassas-Sudley Springs Road, repelling several attacks by Col. Henry Benning's Georgia regiments on their front. Aided by troops from the Fifth Corps and other units gathered to occupy the hill, Reynolds's brigades materially assisted in blunting the force of the Confederate attack.

Reynolds led his division in retreat that evening. Meade's First Brigade had suffered 185 casualties during the battle. Old Baldy was hit in the leg but not seriously hurt. "In a few words," Meade wrote to his wife, "we have been, as usual, *out-manoeuvred* and *out-numbered*, and though not actually defeated, yet compelled to fall on Washington for its defense and our own safety." Meade felt that his conduct in the battle entitled him to command a division. He also warned Margaret that the enemy would probably invade Maryland rather than chance an attack upon the capital. The Reserves, concluded Meade, were "pretty well used up," and should be withdrawn for reorganizing and recruiting.[3]

Chapter 4

Higher Command

A FTER POPE'S beaten troops returned to the Washington defenses, Pope was relieved of command. McClellan was reinstated and given the authority to reorganize the army and defend Maryland against Lee, whose army crossed the Potomac and entered the Old Line State. As part of the army reorganization, McDowell was relieved from corps command and replaced by Hooker. The corps was renumbered as the First Corps, with the divisions commanded by King, Gen. James B. Ricketts, and Reynolds. Meade continued in brigade command.

McClellan took the First, Second, Fifth, Sixth, Ninth, and Twelfth Corps westward to engage Lee. The enemy fell back as the Federals rolled forward. By the time the Pennsylvania Reserves marched into Frederick, Meade was in command of the division. When the Confederates invaded Maryland, Pennsylvania Governor Curtin began agitating for a commander for the state militia that he called up to protect the commonwealth from the enemy. Curtin wanted Reynolds detached for the emergency to command the state troops. Gen. Henry W. Halleck, McClellan, and Hooker all objected, but in the end, Curtin got his way and Reynolds was ordered north to Harrisburg, much to Meade's delight. He was given command of the Reserves when Reynolds departed.

Two days after being elevated to divisional command, Meade saw his first test in battle. McClellan received the now-famous lost orders that detailed Lee's plans. To counter Lee's movements, McClellan directed the Army of the Potomac toward South Mountain and its passes. Stonewall Jackson's corps was besieging the Union garrison at Harper's Ferry while Lee placed Longstreet's troops in the key passes through the mountain range. If McClellan could plow through the passes, he could defeat Lee in detail before Jackson would be able to rejoin his chief.

Accordingly, September 14, 1862, saw action as Union troops assailed South Mountain. Hooker's corps led the attack at Turner's Gap, with Meade's division on the right flank. Hooker and Meade agreed that the Reserves would make the main attack to seize a series of defended ridges up the mountain. Preceded by the Bucktails, Meade's three brigades swept forward, and in an all-day series of fighting, managed to gain the crest of the pass. Casualties totaled some 392, including Col. Thomas F. Gallagher, commanding the Third Brigade, who was wounded.

The army followed the retreating Confederates to the banks of Antietam Creek. There, Lee drew his smaller army behind the creek, defending the small village of Sharpsburg while waiting for Jackson's troops. Harper's Ferry surrendered to the Confederates on September 15 as the two armies filed into line on opposite sides of the creek. Jackson immediately began sending his troops to join Lee, who decided to stay and fight rather than retreat.

McClellan decided to attack the enemy, beginning on Lee's left and extending along the line to the right. On the afternoon of September 16, Hooker's corps forded Antietam Creek and began maneuvering to face Lee's left. As darkness approached, Meade's division became engaged in a fight with elements of Gen. John B. Hood's division in a piece of woods that would go down in history as the East Woods. The Pennsylvanians finally managed to hold the woods, but Col. Hugh McNeil of the Bucktails was killed in the fierce fighting.

The Battle of Antietam opened shortly after dawn on September 17 as Hooker's corps opened the fight by attacking Lee's left, held by some of Jackson's divisions. Meade sent General Seymour's brigade into a large cornfield, then deployed his other two brigades to support the attack. Hooker soon ordered Meade to send a brigade to assist Ricketts's division, whose attack had bogged down in the cornfield. Meade sent in Col. Albert L. Magilton's regiments, managing to stabilize Ricketts's line in short order. After more ferocious fighting in and around the cornfield, Hooker's attack was exhausted. Meade was struck in the thigh by a piece of spent grapeshot, leaving him with a painful bruise. Old Baldy was shot through the neck, but recovered later. Meade left his favorite horse and mounted a cavalry steed to continue the battle.

And then, the general received an unexpected order—he was placed in temporary command of the First Corps after Hooker was hit in the foot and carried from the field. At first Meade thought that the order must be a mistake. General Ricketts was his senior in rank, and surely McClellan must have meant the order for Ricketts. Meade rode quickly to see Ricketts and inform him of Hooker's wounding, and actually turned command of the First Corps over to him, but then two successive orders from McClellan clearly indicated that Meade was to command the corps. The order also stated that Meade was to withdraw the corps, replenish ammunition, reorganize if needed, and be prepared to hold the army's right flank at all costs. Meade followed his orders and managed to reorganize the corps, which was not called upon to reenter the battle.

Lee remained on the battlefield and withdrew across the Potomac River on the evening of September 18. McClellan did not pursue, and chose instead to place the army in camp near the field and begin the process of replenishing the army's supplies and allowing the troops to rest. The Army of the Potomac was still there when President Lincoln visited McClellan in early

October, hoping to goad the general into some type of offensive movement. McClellan took great pride in showing Lincoln over the battlefield. By the time of the President's visit, Reynolds had returned to the Army and assumed command of the corps in Hooker's absence, leaving Meade in division command.

New regiments arrived to bolster the army's strength, and Meade received two of them, the 121st and 142nd Pennsylvania. The Reserves now consisted of three brigades of five regiments each, but severe losses since Mechanicsville had reduced the strength of the division to less than five thousand men. Col. William Sinclair led the First Brigade, Magilton the Second, and Brig. Gen. C. Feger Jackson the Third. The division also had four batteries of artillery attached.

Meade also had to worry about his son George, whose demerits at West Point made him ineligible for final exams. Young George had returned to Philadelphia in late June and was restless, yet too young to enlist without parental consent, which Margaret withheld until assured that he would find a suitable position for a man of his stature. Finally, that fall, young Meade received an appointment to the prestigious Sixth Pennsylvania Cavalry, a Philadelphia unit that contained many officers from blue-blood city families. Known as "Rush's Lancers" after the first colonel, Richard H. Rush, the regiment had originally been equipped with nine-foot lances, which proved to be useless in wooded terrain and were discarded by the time Meade joined the unit. His commission as a second lieutenant in Company B bore the date of November 20, 1862.

By the time that young Meade had entered the Army, his father's division had accompanied the rest of the Army of the Potomac south into Virginia. McClellan finally crossed the Potomac in late October and moved to Warrenton. There, on November 5, McClellan received the startling news that he was relieved of command and replaced with Gen. Ambrose E. Burnside. Meade, in company with Reynolds, Gen. John Gibbon (new Second Division commander), and Gen. Abner Doubleday (Third Division), visited McClellan on November 9 to say their farewells. Although Meade was sympathetic to McClellan's plight, he wrote to his wife that the general's main fault was in waiting too long to attack until everything was just right. As a result, Meade wrote, the enemy usually frustrated McClellan's plans by attacking first. McClellan was too cautious, opined Meade.

Burnside changed the formation of the army by creating three Grand Divisions of two corps each. Reynolds and the First Corps became part of Maj. Gen. William B. Franklin's Left Grand Division, which also included the Sixth Corps. Burnside hoped to sidle the Army of the Potomac southeastward to Fredericksburg, cross the Rappahannock quickly on pontoons sent from Washington, and either force Lee to fight or compel his retreat toward Richmond. The first phase of the march went well, but the pontoons failed to arrive on time and Burnside prohibited his lead troops from crossing to occupy Fredericksburg before the bridges arrived. As a result, Lee managed to catch up and placed his troops on the heights beyond the city, confronting the Army of the Potomac.

In early December, Meade was gratified to be informed of his promotion to major general, effective from November 29. The weather turned cold and the troops had a difficult time while waiting for action. Meade was able to see his son George from time to time, now that the Sixth Pennsylvania Cavalry was in the same area.

Instead of devising another plan, Burnside clung stubbornly to his original idea to cross at Fredericksburg. Once the pontoons arrived, they were placed down under fire and the army crossed on December 11 and 12. Burnside bolstered Franklin's six divisions with three more, giving him almost half the army. Franklin's troops were to assail the enemy position at Hamilton's Crossing and effect a breakthrough, while other attacks along the line would pin down the enemy to prevent reinforcements from reaching Franklin's area of attack.

But Burnside's order to Franklin was garbled and suggested that Franklin need only send one division forward rather than specifying that he attack with his entire strength. Franklin ordered Meade's division to make the main assault on December 13. Reynolds told Meade that Gibbon would support his right and Doubleday would deploy on his left, with the Sixth Corps behind the First.

Meade deployed his Second and Third Brigades in line, supporting them with the First. As the division formed for the assault, Confederate cannon led by the dashing Maj. John Pelham opened an enfilading fire from the left. After some time, Pelham was compelled to withdraw and Meade sent his veterans forward. "I cannot give you all the details of the fight," he wrote to Margaret three days later, "but will simply say my men went in *beautifully*, carried everything before them, and drove the enemy for nearly half a mile, but finding themselves unsupported on either right or left, and encountering an overwhelming force of the enemy, they were checked and finally driven back."[1]

Meade's brigades marched forward over the open ground in front of Stonewall Jackson's line, crossed the line of the Richmond, Fredericksburg & Potomac Railroad, and slammed into A. P. Hill's division posted in the wooded ridge overlooking the Federal advance. The Pennsylvanians drove back two brigades and penetrated a gap in the enemy line caused by some swampy ground. Brig. Gen. Maxcy Gregg, commanding a South Carolina brigade, was killed when he mistakenly believed Meade's oncoming men were friendly troops. But Meade's advance ran out of steam as his units became fragmented in the woods and enemy reinforcements rushed to seal the breakthrough.

Meade himself went through the fight unscathed, except for a bullet that went through his hat. Colonel Sinclair of the First Brigade was wounded, and General Jackson of the Third left dead on the field. Lt. Arthur Dehon, one of Meade's aides, was also killed in the fierce fighting. Angered at the lack of support, Meade rode back to find more troops to help his men. Gen. David Birney, commanding a Third Corps division, claimed he had no orders to advance. Meade, in a huff, ordered Birney forward, but it was too late. Gibbon's division also attacked on

Meade's right, and likewise had to retreat. More troops came to help Hill, and the outnumbered Reserves broke and went to the rear. More Union troops finally came up and helped cover the withdrawal.

Meade had taken perhaps 4,500 men into the attack and lost 1,853, more than 30 percent of the division. As he exclaimed afterward to Reynolds, "Did they think my division could whip Lee's whole army? There is all that is left of my Reserves."[2]

The battle of Fredericksburg was a bitter defeat for Burnside and the Army of the Potomac, which suffered casualties of more than 12,000 against Lee's 5,309. The effects of the battle lowered Union morale and started a series of officer feuds that ended with Burnside's resignation on January 26, 1863. Burnside himself was angry that Franklin had not done more to attack instead of sending in only Meade's division. But Meade's attack showed others in the army that the general was a brave man and a capable commander.

Thinking he wanted to go home on a brief leave, Meade went to visit Burnside shortly after the battle. Burnside told a surprised Meade that he could go home, but also that he wished to promote Meade to command of the Fifth Corps, replacing Porter who was removed for alleged misconduct at Second Manassas. Burnside further said that he would have issued the order immediately, but Hooker, whose grand division included the Fifth Corps, had objected. The general in chief told Meade he was going to Washington to iron out any problems about placing Meade in corps command. Meade thereupon withdrew his leave request.

Burnside returned from Washington on the evening of December 22. The next morning he issued an order placing Meade in command of the Fifth Corps in place of Brig. Gen. Daniel Butterfield, a general junior to Meade but with enough political clout to have garnered the corps command. Meade rode over to Hooker's headquarters on the day before Christmas to report for duty. Hooker tried to assuage Meade's feelings by informing him that there was no other officer in the Army he preferred for corps command, but since Butterfield had discharged his duties competently during the late battle, he felt he must object to his friend Butterfield being displaced.

General Butterfield even invited Meade to have Christmas dinner with him, during which he discussed the matter with Meade. Burnside had told him, said Butterfield, that his appointment to corps command was permanent. Meade sympathized with Butterfield and the two generals smoked cigars while discussing their feelings.

Meade took over a corps associated with the deposed McClellan, since Porter was one of McClellan's staunchest allies. Brig. Gen. Charles Griffin, a Regular Army artillerist, led the First Division. Brig. Gen. George Sykes, another Regular Army officer of long standing led the Second Division, which included two brigades of Regulars. Fellow Pennsylvanian Brig. Gen. Andrew A. Humphreys was in command of two brigades of Pennsylvania regiments that made up the Third Division, which had received its baptism of fire at Fredericksburg.

Meade finally managed to get home for a one-day stay in mid-January, then was called to Washington to testify before the military court trying Porter for his alleged misconduct. Burnside then attempted another campaign by starting the army on a march up the Rappahannock to cross above Lee and attack his flank. The movement started on January 20, but a drizzle began that night, then turned into a major storm that bogged the army down and sent it slogging through mud back to its camps. This "Mud March" as it was known was Burnside's last gasp as army commander. Burnside said he would resign unless other officers were dismissed, but Lincoln accepted his resignation and replaced Burnside with Hooker on January 26.

Hooker, aided by Butterfield, now the general's chief of staff, immediately began to take steps to restore the army's shattered morale. A general pardon was given to all those absent without leave, a new and generous leave policy was established, more food and equipment was stockpiled and distributed, and a system of badges to differentiate each corps was also inaugurated. Meade's Fifth Corps was given a Maltese cross for its badge.

As winter gave way to spring, Hooker devised a plan to force Lee out of his entrenchments behind Fredericksburg. Leaving Reynolds and John Sedgwick to occupy the enemy's attention, Hooker planned to move the rest of the army north along the Rappahannock River several miles above Fredericksburg, cross over, then rapidly move to and cross the Rapidan River. Once across this latter stream, the five army corps would advance through the wilderness area into open ground behind Fredericksburg. Lee would be faced with the choice of giving battle in the open or retreating toward Richmond.

Screened by cavalry, Meade's Fifth Corps left its camps on April 27, leading the five infantry corps designated for the flank movement. Meade's corps began crossing the Rappahannock on the twenty-ninth, using a pontoon bridge at Kelly's Ford. Arriving at the Rapidan, the troops saw that the river was swollen from recent rainstorms. Nevertheless, Meade ordered his corps to cross at Ely's Ford, which had to be waded. The general was cheered by his troops as he sat on Old Baldy and watched the regiments splash across the river. In spite of orders to the contrary, Meade allowed his wet soldiers the luxury of campfires that evening.

The next morning, Meade had his corps moving at first light. Later, Griffin's division emerged into the clearing around the Chancellor house, followed closely by Sykes's troops. By midafternoon, the Fifth Corps was poised to strike eastward toward Fredericksburg. But when Maj. Gen. Henry Slocum, commanding the Twelfth Corps, arrived to Meade's accolades in praise of Hooker's brilliant movement, it was with orders to assume command as the senior general and make no further advance until the Fifth, Eleventh, and Twelfth Corps were all concentrated at Chancellorsville. The Second and Third Corps were also on their way to join Hooker's main force. Griffin's advance troops had already pushed eastward on the Orange Turnpike, encountering the enemy deployed on some high ground at the edge of the wooded country. When Griffin asked for reinforcements to attack, Meade could only order him to return to the Chancellor house area.

Hooker himself reached Chancellorsville later on April 30. On May 1, he asked Meade to send Sykes's division down the Orange Turnpike while Meade accompanied his other two divisions down the road toward Banks's Ford on the Rappahannock. Occupation of this ford would enable reinforcements to reach the army much quicker than moving upriver to United States Ford. When in sight of the ford, Meade received Hooker's order to return to Chancellorsville. Meade here learned that Sykes had advanced and encountered enemy troops, then retired after requesting more support from Hooker, who instead ordered him to retreat.

Hooker spent the next day crafting a defensive line anchored on the Rappahannock and extending past the Chancellor house area westward along the Orange Turnpike. Meade's corps occupied the left of the line. That day, Stonewall Jackson's corps crossed the front of the Union line and late in the afternoon rolled through the forest and overwhelmed the Eleventh Corps, on the Union right flank. Maj. Gen. Daniel E. Sickles, commanding the Third Corps, had earlier advanced to strike at Jackson's column, leaving a gap in the line. So when Jackson's attack struck, there was no support for the Eleventh Corps.

Meade heard the sound of firing on the Union right and surmised that the enemy had attacked and were coming closer to his own position. He sent Sykes to deploy along the road to Ely's Ford to anchor a new line in case the army had to retreat. The general also sent aides to collect as many cannon as possible and massed them to prevent an enemy breakthrough. That night, Jackson was shot by his own men after reconnoitering in front of his lines. Men of both armies got little sleep as Sickles launched a night attack in an effort to clear his way back to the main line.

The fighting resumed at dawn on May 3 as Jackson's troops struck at the Federal positions around Chancellorsville. Meade's corps sat idly by as only part of the army was engaged, waiting for orders from Hooker that never came. Reynolds and the First Corps also arrived on the battlefield and filed into position near Meade's regiments. Yet when Maj. Gen. Darius N. Couch of the Second Corps requested aid, Meade sent in a brigade, which discovered that the enemy had no reserve troops and could be flanked with a determined attack.

The news from his front was enough for Meade. Accompanied by his chief of staff, Col. Alexander S. Webb, Meade located Hooker, lying injured on a cot near his headquarters. The commanding general had been leaning against a pillar on the porch of the Chancellor mansion when it was hit by a cannonball, knocking him down and leaving him partially disabled. Meade urged Hooker to let the First and Fifth Corps attack the enemy flank. Webb, who witnessed the scene, wrote later that "I have never known anyone so vehemently to advise an attack on the field of battle."[3] But Hooker forbade any attacks and even criticized Meade for sending a brigade to Couch.

Hooker soon placed Couch, the senior corps commander, in charge of the army with orders to withdraw to a new line in rear of the original position then being assailed by the Confederates. Even though Sedgwick attacked and captured Marye's Heights at Fredericksburg, Hooker failed to stir the army as it fell back under enemy pressure. The army remained inactive on May 4 as Lee detached troops to confront Sedgwick, who was defeated at Salem Church and fell back on Banks's Ford.

That night, Hooker called his corps commanders to a conference to discuss whether the army should stay and fight or withdraw across the Rappahannock. Hooker and Butterfield left the tent to allow their subordinates to discuss the situation. Meade argued in favor of a daylight attack, worried that the army would not be able to retreat in safety. Reynolds and Gen. Oliver O. Howard agreed, but Sickles thought it better to retreat and play it safe rather than risk losing the army. Couch voted to fight if he would be allowed to select the point of attack.

When the votes were taken after Hooker returned, Howard

and Meade voted to fight, as did Reynolds. Couch voted to retreat because he had lost confidence in Hooker's ability to lead. Sickles also voted to retreat. Slocum, who arrived later, said he would also fight. But Hooker had already made up his mind and announced that the army would retreat. When leaving the meeting, Meade recalled that Hooker approached him and said that he had seen enough of army command, was ready to turn command over to Meade, and wished he had never been born.

And so, on May 5, the wagon trains led the withdrawal. Later in the day rain came down in torrents and threatened the pontoon bridges over the Rappahannock. But the bridges held and the weary troops managed to cross and return to their old camps around Falmouth. The battle of Chancellorsville had cost Hooker 17,287 men, and Lee suffered a loss of 12,764.

As the army tended to its wounded and replaced lost or damaged equipment, the press began analyzing the battle and politicians began to wonder what had happened. Governor Curtin visited both Reynolds and Meade to see how the two Pennsylvania-born corps commanders were doing. Meade wrote to Margaret that Curtin was bitter about Hooker's failure, but Meade attempted to assuage the Governor's worry. The general remarked that he liked Hooker and felt sorry for him, but he clearly had failed to send in his troops at the critical moment and thus missed "a brilliant opportunity of making himself."[4]

Meade assumed that his conversation with Curtin was private and that the Governor would not broadcast it elsewhere. But word of what Meade had told Curtin got back to Hooker and the general soon appeared at Meade's headquarters, demanding to know what he had said to Curtin. Meade kindly reminded his commander that he already knew they differed about the plight of the army on May 4, and that he had the right to air his opinion privately to others. Hooker sought to avoid an open quarrel and agreed that Meade could speak to others about how he felt.

But a *New York Herald* newspaper article further inflamed the simmering feud when the reporter told his readers that four corps commanders favored an attack. Not so, Hooker argued.

Both Reynolds and Meade had not spoken in favor of an attack, but instead said it was impossible to retreat under the circumstances. Incensed by Hooker's sleight of hand, Meade could only let off steam to his wife.

When Couch asked Meade to join a coalition of other commanders to have Hooker removed from command, Meade refused. However, said Meade, if Lincoln should ask privately his opinion, he would be happy to give it to the President. Still, Couch told Lincoln that he no longer wished to serve under Hooker, and recommended Meade for the position. Others had the same opinion, but when Margaret heard the rumors that her husband would be the next army commander, she warned him not to accept. Meade could only agree with his wife. "I think I know myself, and am sincere when I say I do not desire the command; hence I can quietly attend to my duties, uninfluenced by what is going on around me, at the same time expressing, as I feel, great gratification that the army and my senior generals should think so well of my services and capacity as to be willing to serve under me."[5]

Meade did send a circular letter to his fellow corps commanders, seeking their recollections of the May 4 council of war and what he had said regarding the army's position. Except for Sickles, who claimed that Meade later changed his mind and voted to retreat, all the other commanders remembered that Meade voted to attack. Since no investigations were made, Meade kept the replies confidential, but Sickles had his reply printed in the *Herald*. Clearly, Meade had made some enemies, and rumors swirled that he might be removed from corps command. Meade opined that if he was removed, the other commanders should also be penalized for their thoughts on the battle. In spite of such differences, Meade believed that Hooker still had merit and might perform better in another battle.

As Lee strengthened and reorganized the Army of Northern Virginia, the Army of the Potomac began losing troops as many nine-month and two-year regiments began mustering out. Meade lost an entire division; his Third Division was composed primarily of short-term Pennsylvania regiments that went home, leaving Humphreys without a command. Humphreys was soon transferred to the Third Corps, replacing Hiram G. Berry, who had been killed at Chancellorsville, where he was in command of Sickles's Second Division. The Fifth Corps was thus reduced to two divisions.

Lee's army began leaving the Fredericksburg area on June 3, heading toward the Shenandoah Valley and a projected move north of the Potomac River into Maryland and Pennsylvania. After the cavalry battle at Brandy Station on June 9, Hooker began to move the Army of the Potomac north to stay between Lee and Washington, generally paralleling the enemy line of march. Cavalry engagements erupted when Hooker's mounted troops sparred with Stuart's horsemen in the Bull Run Mountains as both sides tried to keep each other's horsemen from locating the marching infantry units.

By nightfall on June 27, Meade's Fifth Corps went into bivouac just south of Frederick, Maryland. The general was in an irritable mood that night. He had not seen Hooker for more than two weeks and had no idea what was happening. Hooker had kept his plans secret and his corps commanders were left wondering where the enemy was and what Hooker intended to do. Meade could not have known that Hooker had tendered his resignation earlier that day. Hooker had squabbled with Lincoln's general in chief, Halleck, over the Harper's Ferry garrison. Hooker wanted to add it to the field army, even after receiving some reinforcements from the Washington defenses. When Halleck refused, Hooker asked to be relieved.

Secretary of War Edwin Stanton met with Lincoln early that evening and told the President that Hooker was not equal to the present emergency and ought to be removed from command. Meade, said Stanton, should replace Hooker. Lincoln agreed and called in Halleck, who wrote out the necessary orders. Col. James A. Hardie of the War Department boarded a train to Frederick to deliver the order to Meade in person.

Hardie arrived in Frederick sometime after midnight. No one

seemed to know where Meade's corps was camped, but Hardie eventually managed to hire a driver and buggy. After searching through the darkness for quite some time, they located the Fifth Corps encampment. At about three o'clock on the morning of June 28, Colonel Hardie walked into Meade's tent without making his mission known to Meade's staff officers.

Meade's first reaction upon being awakened by Colonel Hardie was to assume that he was under arrest because of his differences with General Hooker. But then Hardie gave the surprised Meade the order assigning him to command of the Army of the Potomac. Hardie also gave Meade a letter from Halleck that outlined his duties. Above all, Meade was to ensure the safety of Washington. If Lee moved on either Baltimore or Philadelphia, Meade was expected to intercept the Confederates and fight a battle. All troops within the army's sphere of operations were placed under Meade's command, including the Harper's Ferry garrison. Halleck also authorized Meade to "remove from command, and to send from your army, any officer or other person you may deem proper, and to appoint to command as you may deem expedient."[6]

Meade and Hardie then visited Hooker, who had already guessed Hardie's mission once he learned of the colonel's presence. Before leaving, Hooker briefed Meade on the army's location and what he knew of Lee's troops. At seven o'clock on the morning of June 28, Meade wired a telegram to Halleck, advising him that he had received the order and would execute it "to the utmost of my ability."[7] Meade planned to move the army toward the Susquehanna River, keeping between Lee and Baltimore, and would fight Lee once he turned away from the river.

Chapter 5

Gettysburg

MEADE QUICKLY ISSUED orders that were de-
signed to concentrate the army in the vicinity of Frederick. By
nightfall, all seven infantry corps were within ten miles of the
city, thus bringing the corps within supporting distance of each
other. During the day, Meade also sounded out three candidates
for the chief of staff position. Butterfield had been Hooker's
chief of staff, but Meade felt that he wanted someone he could
trust. He approached A. General Humphreys, commanding one
of Sickles's divisions; Adjutant General Seth Williams; and Chief
Engineer Gouverneur K. Warren. All three advised Meade that
Butterfield was the best man for the job under the circumstances
of an active military campaign. Meade reluctantly accepted this
conclusion and decided to stick with Butterfield.

The orders for June 29, 1863, reflected Meade's decision to
head for Lee's army and abandon Hooker's idea of striking at the
enemy communications. Although Maj. Gen. Winfield S. Hancock's and Slocum's corps did not reach their objectives, by
nightfall the army was lined up between Emmitsburg and New
Windsor, Maryland. Meade also ordered Maj. Gen. William H.

French, commanding at Harper's Ferry, to remove all military stores and march to join the army with most of his troops.

June 30 saw Meade transfer his headquarters to Taneytown, Maryland, as the left wing under Reynolds neared the Mason-Dixon Line and the Fifth Corps crossed the border to Littlestown, Pennsylvania. Brig. Gen. John Buford's cavalry had entered the crossroads town of Gettysburg in Adams County, Pennsylvania, and located Confederate infantry to the west. By the thirtieth, Meade believed that his rapid advance to the Pennsylvania border had forced Lee to turn back from the Susquehanna, making a battle imminent as his units began concentrating somewhere west of Gettysburg. As a result, Meade began to search for a battlefield. Engineer officers had suggested defending the line of Pipe Creek, Maryland, which provided a good position for fighting a defensive battle. Meade sent Brig. Gen. Henry J. Hunt, his chief of artillery, and Warren to survey this line as a possible battlefield.

Early the next morning, July 1, Meade telegraphed to Halleck some general information on the Confederate positions and a brief note about the Pipe Creek Line, concluding with the statement that if Lee did not attack, and if he could obtain reliable information about the enemy, he would launch an attack on the enemy. Meade sent orders to his corps commanders to concentrate behind Pipe Creek, especially if Lee attacked.

However, by the time Meade sent out this "Pipe Creek Circular," it was obsolete. Maj. Gen. Henry Heth's Confederate division had moved toward Gettysburg and engaged Buford's dismounted troopers. Advised of the situation, General Reynolds hastened to Gettysburg, his corps following. Once at Gettysburg, Reynolds decided to support Buford and sent orders to Howard and Sickles to hasten forward with their troops. As he led the Iron Brigade into battle, Reynolds was struck by a minié ball and killed.

At 11:20 that morning, Capt. Stephen M. Weld arrived at army headquarters with a note for Meade from Reynolds. The First Corps commander advised Meade that the enemy was advancing in force and that he would fight them "inch by inch" and hold them back as long as possible. Shortly thereafter, a courier from Buford arrived, confirming the fact that the enemy was moving on Gettysburg.

Based on this information, Meade began making some revisions to the Pipe Creek orders in case Reynolds had to fall back. But at one o'clock, Maj. William Riddle arrived at army headquarters with the sad news of Reynolds's death. Only ten minutes later, Meade ordered Hancock, whose Second Corps was bivouacked nearby, to proceed to Gettysburg and assume command of all the troops assembled there. Meade told Hancock that he was to examine the field there, and if it seemed a good place to fight a battle, he was to so inform Meade, who would then order the army to Gettysburg.

Once Hancock left for Gettysburg, Meade could only await further developments. Dispatches from Howard and Buford were maddeningly terse, but Meade was already contemplating moving the rest of the army to Gettysburg, and so informed Halleck of his decision. Sometime after six o'clock, one of Hancock's staff officers arrived with information about the battle and the fact that Hancock would hold the ground until dark to allow Meade time to make his decision. An hour later, Capt. Israel B. Parker arrived with a lengthy note from Hancock, who reported that "the ground appears not unfavorable with good troops."[1]

Meade had already sent out orders to all corps commanders to march for Gettysburg. He hoped to assemble the army there and perhaps attack the Confederates before they were fully concentrated. Meade left Taneytown and arrived at the Gettysburg Cemetery gatehouse shortly after midnight where Generals Howard, Slocum, and Sickles were assembled. Meade heard their opinions of the ground and about the day's battle, in which the Union First and Eleventh Corps had been driven through Gettysburg and rallied on the high ground south of town.

Later, before dawn, Meade undertook a reconnaissance of the area. Accompanied by Generals Hunt and Howard, and Capt. William H. Paine of the engineers, Meade was able to survey the positions of the troops and decide on a line of battle. Captain

Paine was ordered to make copies of the rough sketch map he drew and send a copy to each corps commander, noting where each corps was to go into position.

Once he finished giving orders to his subordinates, Meade located his headquarters in the Widow Leister farmhouse, located along the Taneytown Road behind the approximate center of the proposed line. When completed, the Union line formed what has been called a fishhook shape, beginning on the right at Culp's Hill, extending west to Cemetery Hill, then south along Cemetery Ridge to the Round Tops, two prominent hills that were easily seen on the southern horizon. Maj. Gen. Alfred Pleasonton would cover both flanks with his cavalry.

During the day on July 2, the Army of the Potomac continued to move to Gettysburg. The Second Corps arrived early in the morning, and two divisions of the Fifth Corps arrived behind the right flank around eight o'clock. An hour later, two Third Corps brigades left behind at Emmitsburg reached the field. Two brigades of the Pennsylvania Reserves, released from the Washington defenses, reached the field about noon and were assigned to the Fifth Corps. The army's largest corps, Sedgwick's Sixth, was en route to the battlefield from Manchester, Maryland, more than thirty miles away. Maj. Gen. John Newton, whom Meade ordered forward from Sedgwick's corps to assume command of the First Corps in lieu of Reynolds, reported to Meade that Sedgwick was pushing his men as fast as possible and would arrive later that afternoon.

Sometime between six and seven o'clock, General Meade sent his son George, recently promoted to captain and assigned to his staff as an aide, to visit General Sickles to make sure that the Third Corps was in position and to see if Sickles had anything to report. Sickles had been assigned to form his two divisions on Hancock's left and extend the line south along Cemetery Ridge to Little Round Top, which he was to occupy if practicable. When Captain Meade rode up to Third Corps headquarters, he found that the corps was not yet in position because Sickles was in some doubt about where his corps was supposed to be.

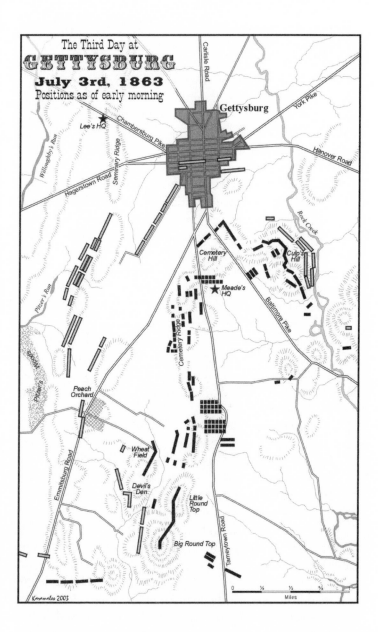

The Third Day at
GETTYSBURG
July 3rd, 1863
Positions as of early morning

Gettysburg

Carlisle Road

York Pike

Hanover Road

Lee's HQ

Chambersburg Pike

Willoughby's Run

Hagerstown Road

Seminary Ridge

Rock Creek

Cemetery Hill

Culp's Hill

Meade's HQ

Pitzer's Run

Baltimore Pike

Cemetery Ridge

PITZER'S WOODS

Peach Orchard

Wheat Field

Devil's Den

Little Round Top

Emmitsburg Road

Taneytown Road

Big Round Top

Karamales 2003

0   ¼   ½   ¾
Miles

Surprised at this answer, Captain Meade reported to his father what he heard. Visibly annoyed at hearing this, General Meade ordered his son to advise Sickles that he was to form on Hancock's left and occupy the line held by Brig. Gen. John W. Geary's Twelfth Corps division the night before, and do this as soon as possible. Once Meade rode south for a return visit, he found Sickles, who said his troops were moving and would be in position. Sickles added that Geary's men seemed to have had no discernible position.

While Sickles hesitated to deploy his corps, Meade was trying to find out more about Lee's positions. Based on visual evidence, it seemed that the enemy was concentrating opposite the Federal right. Slocum and Warren undertook a reconnaissance of the terrain in front of Culp's Hill to see if the army might attack the enemy with a chance of success, but Meade was dissuaded from this notion when he heard their unfavorable report; the terrain would hinder an attack by either side.

Meade thus decided to await Lee's movements. The Army of the Potomac had marched long and hard to reach Gettysburg and the troops were tired. Once the Sixth Corps arrived, Meade would have enough troops for an attack. The morning warmed up as a typical hot July day, punctuated by skirmish fire along the lines of battle.

Sometime around eleven that morning, Sickles appeared at headquarters and announced that he was unsure of the position his corps was supposed to occupy. Meade repeated his earlier instructions, pointing out Little Round Top on the horizon. Meade authorized General Hunt to accompany Sickles and examine possible artillery positions.

Sickles took Hunt out to Emmitsburg Road, which generally followed the crest of a small ridge midway between the two armies. This higher ground dominated the lower end of Cemetery Ridge. Sickles feared that Confederate occupation of this area would compromise the location of his corps. Would Hunt give him permission to move the Third Corps forward to this line? Hunt wisely demurred; he told Sickles he would report the situation to Meade. Hunt also suggested that Sickles send a reconnaissance force out into a belt of woods in front of the proposed line to scout for enemy soldiers.

Sickles acted on Hunt's suggestion by sending out Col. Hiram Berdan with four companies of his sharpshooters and the Third Maine as a support. Berdan's men encountered part of Brig. Gen. Cadmus Wilcox's Alabama Brigade, which was moving into position in Pitzer's Woods. Berdan reported the ensuing skirmish to Sickles, who believed that a Confederate force was moving across his front to outflank his corps.

In actuality, Wilcox's men were a part of Maj. Gen. Richard Anderson's division of A. P. Hill's Third Corps and were moving into position to await further events. General Lee had decided to attack the Union left, which he mistakenly believed only extended partway south along Cemetery Ridge; his scouts had failed to see Sickles's corps, which was hidden by trees and some morning fog. Thus, he ordered Longstreet, his First Corps commander, to move his two available divisions into position at the Peach Orchard and attack "up the Emmitsburg Road." Hill's troops would join the attack as it progressed to their positions. Lt. Gen. Richard S. Ewell's Second Corps would attack Culp's Hill to prevent reinforcements from moving to Meade's left. If all went well, Lee's attacks would drive the Yankees from their strong position.

As Longstreet moved his divisions into position, Sickles, worried over Berdan's report, decided to assume the responsibility of moving his troops forward to the Emmitsburg Road. Shortly after two o'clock, Sickles's two divisions moved forward, Humphreys occupying a line along the Emmitsburg Road, while David Birney's division anchored its left in the Devil's Den area and its right at the Peach Orchard. When thus deployed, Sickles's corps formed a V-shaped salient with no support at either end.

General Meade did not learn of Sickles's unauthorized move until sometime after three o'clock, when he called his corps commanders to his headquarters for a conference. By the time Sickles arrived, the sound of artillery was heard from the direction of Sickles's line. One of Warren's engineer officers reported that affairs were amiss on Sickles's front. Meade broke up the intended conference and rode off to see what had happened, sending orders to Sykes to bring the Fifth Corps over to the left as soon as possible.

Meade caught up with Sickles in rear of the Peach Orchard. After Sickles pointed out his new line, Meade, known throughout the Army for his temper, exploded with rage at Sickles's unauthorized move. Meade reprimanded the political general for not realizing that the Emmitsburg Road ridge was neutral ground; neither army would be able to hold the ground for any length of time. Sickles, apparently sorry for misconstruing his orders, offered to move his corps back to Cemetery Ridge. Meade so ordered, but just then Longstreet's artillery opened a massed fire. Meade told Sickles to remain in position and that he would send reinforcements.

As Meade left Sickles, he ordered Warren, who had accompanied him, to ride to the left of the line and investigate the situation. Warren made his way to the summit of Little Round Top, unoccupied except for a detachment of the signal corps. Warren quickly realized that the hill was the key to the Federal position at Gettysburg; if seized by the enemy, Meade would be forced to retreat. Warren also detected Longstreet's men moving into position and saw at once that they overlapped Sickles's flank. He quickly sent aides in search of reinforcements. Col. Strong Vincent's Fifth Corps brigade arrived on the hill only moments before Southern troops from Hood's division began advancing up its southern slope.

Meade spent several stressful hours receiving reports and coordinating the movement of his army. Sickles's position and Longstreet's attack meant that Meade did not have the luxury of time to build a new defensive line. Instead, troops arrived piecemeal and were fed into battle as they arrived on Sickles's front. By the time the fighting died out after dark, the entire Fifth Corps had become engaged, as well as five brigades from the Second

Corps, three Twelfth Corps brigades, two depleted First Corps divisions, and some of the fatigued Sixth Corps. Other parts of the line were dangerously weakened, but the uncoordinated Confederate assaults on Cemetery Ridge and Culp's Hill failed to take advantage of the situation. Sickles's corps was driven back and by nightfall, the Union line on Cemetery Ridge was occupied by massed brigades ready to oppose a further enemy attack.

Once the fighting died down, Meade again ordered his corps commanders to assemble at army headquarters to assess the situation. In addition to the corps commanders, Butterfield and Warren were present, as were General Gibbon and Brig. Gen. Alpheus S. Williams, division commanders temporarily acting as corps commanders. The conference allowed Meade's generals to listen to each other's reports, assess casualties, and talk about future strategy. Butterfield, with Meade's assent, placed three questions before the council: 1) is it advisable for the army to remain in position? 2) If so, should the army attack or defend? and 3) If they await attack, how long? All the generals agreed to remain in position and defend against the Confederates, with a variety of answers as to how long to wait.

Meade had already sent a telegram to Halleck outlining the day's fighting and his decision to remain and allow the Confederates to continue to attack his strong position. The "council of war" merely reaffirmed his decision to stay and fight at Gettysburg. As General Gibbon was leaving the house, Meade pulled him aside and told him that if Lee attacked tomorrow, it would be against his position. When asked why, Meade replied that Lee's flank attacks had failed, and he suspected that Lee would launch a major attack against the center of the line.

Indeed, Lee decided to launch a massive attack on Meade's center, since assaults on both flanks had been repelled. Ewell would continue to attack on Culp's Hill, while Stuart's cavalry would attempt to get in the Federal rear, creating chaos and distracting the enemy from the planned frontal attack.

Meade also authorized Slocum to launch a dawn attack to drive the Confederates out of some entrenchments they had occupied on the slopes of Culp's Hill. The next morning, Meade rode off to the right and witnessed the opening of Slocum's attack. He then rode south along the line, occasionally stopping to chat with subordinates. Meade eventually wound up on Little Round Top with Warren, noting the massing batteries of Confederate cannon that stretched north from the Peach Orchard along Seminary Ridge.

At lunchtime, General Gibbon visited headquarters and found Meade looking "worn and haggard." Gibbon invited Meade to lunch with him; one of his servants had located an old rooster and stewed it. A few other officers joined the general, who lit a cigar and discussed Confederate options. Meade apparently now thought that Lee would again attack on the Union left. An attack on Hancock's position in the center would be suicidal, given the excellent fields of fire for the fine Union artillery. After relaxing a bit, Meade returned to headquarters.

Shortly after one o'clock, the massed Confederate batteries began firing at the Union center. As infantrymen scurried for cover and Union cannon began to reply, smoke obscured the battlefield. Unfortunately for the Confederates, much of their artillery fire flew harmlessly over Cemetery Ridge to explode on the reverse slope of the ridge. As a result, the Leister house received a pummeling. Indeed, Meade and his staff were extremely lucky to avoid casualties. The general himself was standing in the doorway to the house when a solid shot crashed into a nearby box, grazing him slightly.

Meade was reluctant to move because he needed to remain where messengers could find him. He did consent to move outside to avoid flying splinters, one of which wounded General Butterfield. Amused at his staff's efforts to find a safe spot, Meade continued to send messages to his generals as he ordered reinforcements to the center of the line. Finally, Meade left the Leister house area and went to Powers Hill after being informed that Slocum's headquarters there had a signal officer who could assist in keeping communications open. But that officer was unable to signal to the officer who was supposed to remain behind at the Leister house, so Meade decided to return to his head-quarters.

By the time Meade returned to the Leister house, the artillery bombardment had stopped and heavy musketry could be heard straight ahead on Cemetery Ridge. Thick smoke hid the state of affairs, so Meade, accompanied by his son, rode toward the ridge to see what was happening. The two men rode into a large body of Confederate prisoners, who saw the general and asked him where they should go. Now in fine spirits, Meade pointed to the rear and laughingly told them they would be well taken care of.

Meade then encountered Lt. Frank A. Haskell, one of Gibbon's aides, who told the general that the Confederates had been repulsed. "What?" an incredulous Meade retorted, "Is the assault entirely repulsed?" As the smoke cleared, Meade could see that Haskell was right. All the relieved Meade could say was "Thank God." His more spirited son threw his cap into the air and loudly huzzahed.[2]

Meade also found out that both Hancock and Gibbon had been wounded during the repulse of Pickett's Charge. Satisfied that the enemy had indeed been repelled, Meade rode north to Cemetery Hill to assess the situation from that area. The general, followed by his staff, then rode south all the way to Little Round Top, receiving the cheers of his victorious army all the way. Although the Confederates saw and heard the cheering, they took no action and no shots were fired at the mounted group of men.

That night, Meade and his staff slept in a small patch of woods near the Taneytown Road. A late-night thunderstorm drenched the party, but the Leister house had been badly damaged and sixteen horses lay dead outside the structure. Meade could congratulate himself on the fine job he had done since receiving command of the army only six days previously. Although the Army of the Potomac had suffered more than 23,000 casualties in the three-day battle of Gettysburg, Lee's smaller army had lost at least 28,000 men, severely crippling the enemy. But Meade had lost Reynolds, who was killed, and both Hancock and Sickles wounded—three of his seven infantry corps commanders. Many brigade and regimental commanders had also been killed, wounded, or captured. Battered but victorious, the Army of the Potomac and its new commander had finally achieved a victory over Robert E. Lee and his Army of Northern Virginia.

Chapter 6

From Gettysburg to Grant

JULY 4, 1863, brought a misty cloud cover to the battlefield at Gettysburg. Occasional picket firing broke out along
the lines, but no major fighting erupted. Both armies were
fought out and tired. Dead bodies had to be buried, dead horses
burned, and wounded men tended to. Lee withdrew from the
Federal right and drew up his army just west of Gettysburg, allowing Yankee patrols to occupy the town. Meade rejected Lee's
proposal to exchange prisoners in order to increase Lee's supply
problems; perhaps 5,000 captured Yankees needed to be fed and
had to be guarded. That night, as rain again began, Meade's
corps commanders met and decided to hold their position until
Lee either retreated or else changed his own position.

Lee's army began to retreat that night, taking routes through
the South Mountain passes toward Williamsport, Maryland. Later
on the fourth, Meade received news from General French that the
First New York Cavalry had raided to the west from Harper's Ferry
and destroyed Lee's pontoon bridge across the Potomac near
Williamsport. Thus, if the rain continued and the Potomac's water level rose, Lee might be unable to cross back into Virginia.

Federal pursuit began late on July 5 when the Sixth Corps moved to follow Lee directly. The rest of the army moved south into Maryland, slowed by muddy roads and continuing rain. Meanwhile, news of the victory at Gettysburg cheered people all across the North. The public scrambled to obtain photos of the victorious Meade, who received messages of congratulations from Generals McClellan and Pope. News of Maj. Gen. Ulysses S. Grant's success at Vicksburg, Mississippi, further aroused Northern spirits. Now, concluded Lincoln, if Meade could destroy Lee's beaten army, the rebellion might be crushed.

As Meade's tired and muddy soldiers marched south, the general received news that he had been promoted to brigadier general in the Regular Army, to rank from July 3, 1863. Although his name continued to receive praise across the North, Meade was also stung by telegrams from General Halleck, who was parroting Lincoln's concern that Lee would escape before the Army of the Potomac could catch up. According to Halleck, Lincoln hoped that the army would move by "forced marches" against the enemy.[1] In reply to this particularly offensive note, Meade said that his army was short of rations and many soldiers were shoeless. Even so, Meade said, the army was continuing to advance toward Williamsport. On July 9, owing to Butterfield's absence because of his wound, Meade took the opportunity to replace him with General Humphreys, who at last consented to leave his division to help manage the army.

As the army neared Williamsport, the advance troops made contact with Lee's men, entrenched in a semicircular position that covered Williamsport. The Potomac River was flooding and it appeared that a decisive Federal attack might bring the desired destruction of Lee's army. Rain late in the day on July 12 frustrated Meade's plan for an attack. The general called a meeting of his corps commanders that night. He declared to them that he favored an immediate attack without taking the time to properly survey the enemy line. But only two of his officers supported such a rash move, so Meade decided to spend the day on July 13 surveying the enemy position and choosing the points of attack for July 14.

But Lee frustrated the Union plans by withdrawing his army that very night, using cobbled-together pontoon bridges to cross the flooded Potomac. When the Yankees moved forward the next morning, they encountered only empty fortifications. Still, Heth's division was bloodied as it acted as rear guard near Falling Waters, Maryland. But when the veterans of the Army of the Potomac—officers and men alike—marched in pursuit and examined the abandoned entrenchments, they felt that an attack would have failed miserably. Lee's engineers had constructed fortifications that took advantage of the terrain and would have repulsed a determined Union attack. General Howard, who had originally voted to attack, wrote that it was "by no means certain that the repulse of Gettysburg might not have been turned against us."[2]

President Lincoln, bitterly disappointed at Lee's escape, penned a vituperative letter that revealed his despair over Meade's inability to bring the war to an end by destroying Lee's army. But the President never sent this missive to Meade and instead laid it aside. Still, Halleck, as usual, trumpeted Lincoln's disappointment in a telegram to Meade. Halleck, on July 14, wrote that an active and energetic pursuit was the order of the day. In response, Meade sent a terse statement of the facts as he saw them: "Having performed my duty conscientiously and to the best of my ability, the censure of the President conveyed in your dispatch of 1 p.m. this day, is, in my judgment, so undeserved that I feel compelled most respectfully to ask to be immediately relieved from the command of this army."[3]

Although Halleck replied in softened tone and said that no censure was implied, Meade believed that he would never be allowed a free hand by the authorities in Washington. Meade recognized that his own "phlegmatic" disposition would get in the way of working with those who misunderstood military matters.

Meade still pressed his army forward and crossed the Potomac at Harper's Ferry on July 15. Newspaper articles brought to

Meade's attention showed that editors across the North were beginning to wonder why Lee had managed to escape. Dan Sickles, recuperating from his wound, told his story of the battle of Gettysburg to all those who would listen. But Meade had his supporters within the Army, and General Howard, at least, wrote a personal letter to the President, in which he declared that Meade was the primary reason there had been a victory at Gettysburg. Everything was done at the right moment, wrote Howard, and always with the hearty cooperation of his subordinates. Howard's defense of his chief brought Lincoln to realize that Meade was indeed a "skillful officer and a true man."[4]

Once the army crossed into Virginia, Meade kept it on the east side of the Blue Ridge Mountains, ready to move in case Lee backtracked and tried to go north again. But Lee continued to retreat and Meade followed. On July 21, Meade sent General French, now commanding the Third Corps, across the mountains in an attempt to interdict the enemy retreat. Had French been more forceful and prompt, the Confederate army might have been cut in half. But French was delayed by a smaller Confederate force on July 22, and Lee's army slipped away once again. The fighting at Wapping Heights clearly showed that French was not Hancock or Reynolds.

Lee continued his retreat until he was safely behind the Rappahannock River. By the beginning of August, the Gettysburg Campaign was over and the two armies glared at each other across the river. Meade concentrated his army around Warrenton and deployed some of his troops to watch the Rappahannock fords as Lee withdrew behind the Rapidan, leaving the triangle of land between the rivers as neutral ground that the cavalry of both sides contested.

Meade wanted to advance against Lee's army, but whenever he and Humphreys drew up plans and presented them to Halleck and Lincoln, they were turned down as too risky. Above all, Meade needed to protect Washington, but at the same time he was supposed to do what he could to push Lee deeper into Virginia. But Meade's army was shrinking. Following the battle of

Gettysburg, the War Department instituted a draft to raise re-placements for the depleted regiments in service. Antidraft riots broke out in New York, forcing the administration to ask Meade for help. The general initially dispatched 1,600 troops, but by the time more were sent to maintain law and order, perhaps 10,000 soldiers had left the Army of the Potomac.

Meade soon heard rumors that Lee was detaching troops to assist Gen. Braxton Bragg's retreating army in Tennessee. Union Maj. Gen. William S. Rosecrans, in the brilliant Tullahoma Campaign, had forced Bragg out of Tennessee and occupied Chattanooga without fighting a battle. As Rosecrans continued his advance into northern Georgia, the Davis administration looked everywhere for additional soldiers to reinforce Bragg. Lee sent General Longstreet and two of his divisions, which left the Army of Northern Virginia on September 7–8.

Meade, reacting to these rumors, sent Pleasonton and his cav-alry across the Rappahannock on September 13. The Yankee horsemen pushed Stuart's cavalry back and occupied Culpeper as Union infantry marched in support. Meade's entire army fol-lowed as the enemy withdrew across the Rapidan and en-trenched, watching the Yankees in their front. Once in control of Culpeper, Meade and Humphreys began planning a further advance designed to outflank Lee's entrenchments behind the Rapidan.

But even as Meade sent his cavalry to investigate where Lee was weakest, he was ordered to Washington on September 21 to confer with administration officials. Meade learned that Longstreet's troops had reached Bragg in time to fight in the two-day battle of Chickamauga on September 19–20. Long-street's opportune arrival tipped the fighting in favor of the Con-federates, and Rosecrans was driven back to Chattanooga. Lincoln, Stanton, and Halleck needed to find reinforcements to send to Rosecrans. After conferring with Meade, it was decided to send both the Eleventh and Twelfth Corps to Chattanooga. General Hooker was brought back on active duty and assigned to the command of these reinforcements, which would leave immediately by rail for Bridgeport, Alabama, the closest railhead to Chattanooga in Union hands.

The detachment of two corps from Meade's command meant that the general had to shelve his plans for an attack on Lee. By early October, however, the troops sent to New York had returned and the army had also begun to receive drafted men to replace losses from the veteran regiments. Thus reinforced, Meade revived his plan to turn one of Lee's flanks.

But Lee began to move before Meade was able to finalize his plans. Lee had learned about the westward movement of Meade's two corps and thus decided upon an offensive designed to push the Yankee army back toward Washington. Starting on October 6, Lee began to sidle his infantry westward along the Rapidan, planning a move to march around Meade's right flank in a campaign similar to Stonewall Jackson's march in August 1862. Meade's signal officers caught glimpses of marching columns and so informed Meade, who shifted the Second Corps west of Culpeper to strengthen his flank.

Rainfall slowed Lee's advance as cavalry fighting erupted in front of the marching columns. General Pleasonton believed that Lee was masking a retreat, and Meade decided to test this hypothesis by sending Buford's cavalry across the Rapidan. At the same time, Meade decided to play it safe by withdrawing his infantry behind the Rappahannock, just in case Lee was trying to outmaneuver him. On October 12, though, Meade sent Sedgwick with two corps back across the Rappahannock to investigate the whereabouts of Lee's army. He planned to follow with the rest of the army if Sedgwick made contact with enemy infantry. Later in the day, the Second Corps followed Sedgwick.

By nightfall, however, Union cavalry confirmed that Confederate infantry had crossed the Rappahannock north of Meade's right flank and thus threatened his communications with Washington. Meade thereupon ordered Sedgwick to withdraw his three corps even as the remaining two corps began to head north to get ahead of Lee's advance. Meade decided to withdraw to

Centreville, where the army would entrench and await a battle with Lee's advancing troops.

General Warren, commanding the Second Corps during Hancock's absence, brought up the rear of the retreating Federals. Brig. Gen. David M. Gregg's cavalry also protected the rear of the infantry column. The corps crossed the Rappahannock and kept plodding along, reaching within a mile of the small village of Auburn after darkness on the thirteenth. The next morning, Warren's men crossed a small stream called Cedar Run and encountered some of Stuart's men in their path, including the general himself. As Brig. Gen. Alexander Hays's division traded shots with the enemy, troops from Ewell's corps began fighting with Gregg's horsemen, placing the Yankees in a trying situation. But Warren's infantry opened the road to Catlett's Station and the corps managed to escape being surrounded.

Later that afternoon, as the corps approached Bristoe Station on the Orange & Alexandria Railroad, the Yankee advance spied troops from A. P. Hill's corps moving into position and skirmishing with the rear guard of Sykes's Fifth Corps. The resulting battle brought the Second Corps into line behind the railroad embankment. Heth's division of Hill's corps attacked and was bloodily repelled, suffering 1,361 casualties. Warren continued his withdrawal and caught up with the Army of the Potomac at Centreville, where the entire army deployed and entrenched.

Although Lee had managed to force Meade to withdraw, the Bristoe Station Campaign, as it has been called, solved nothing. Meade received much criticism for withdrawing in the face of a numerically smaller enemy. As usual, Halleck sent telegrams that were not worded in the most appropriate manner. On October 18, Halleck wrote that "Lee is unquestionably bullying you. . . . If you pursue and fight him, I think you will find out where he is." In reply, Meade showed his anger at receiving such messages. "If you have any orders to give me, I am prepared to receive and obey them, but I must insist on being spared the infliction of such truisms in the guise of opinions. . . . I take this occasion to repeat what I have before stated, that if my course, based on my own judgment, does not meet with approval, I ought to be, and I desire to be, relieved from command."[5]

Halleck again apologized by saying that he was merely repeating the wishes of the government and did not wish to offend Meade. In the meantime, rain called a halt to active military operations. Lee saw that Meade's entrenched army was impossible to assault, so he began a withdrawal, destroying the railroad as his troops fell back behind the Rappahannock River. The Army of the Potomac followed, going into camp around Warrenton as crews began the laborious process of rebuilding the railroad track.

By early November, Meade was ready to advance. Dividing the army into two columns led by Generals French and Sedgwick, Meade edged the army toward the Rappahannock. On November 7, elements of the Sixth Corps charged and captured Lee's bridgehead at Rappahannock Station, taking more than 1,500 prisoners in the brief fighting. French's column crossed at Kelly's Ford, and Lee fell back to his old entrenchments behind the Rapidan River.

Later that month, Meade tried to maneuver Lee out of his entrenchments and force a battle before winter weather could halt active operations. In essence, Meade hoped to move forward rapidly and turn Lee's right flank before the Gray Fox could concentrate his army. After a delay caused by rain, the Mine Run Campaign began on November 26, when the lead units of the Army of the Potomac began crossing the Rapidan downstream from Lee's right. General French's Third Corps moved slowly and derailed Meade's aggressive plan. French was dilatory again on November 27, leaving Warren's corps unsupported as it advanced toward the Confederate right. The delays allowed Ewell's men to fall back behind Mine Run and entrench as the Yankees advanced.

Frustrated, Meade decided to try to turn Ewell's right. He sent Warren, reinforced by three additional divisions, to make the attempt. At first glance, Warren perceived that the enemy entrenchments in his front were not strong. The attack was sched-

uled for the morning of November 28. But Warren, after study-
ing the enemy line and realizing that the Confederates had
strengthened it during the night, called off the attack and sent a
courier to Meade. The general came forward and saw the true
state of affairs. He agreed with Warren's decision. The bitterly
cold weather and rain made conditions bad for the troops, but
for Meade, there would be no useless sacrifice just to appease
those in Washington who wanted action.

During the evening of December 1, Meade's army slipped
away and returned to its camps near Culpeper. Soldiers who expected to be sacrificed were relieved and expressed great praise
for a commander who refused to waste lives. Lt. Col. Theodore
Lyman, one of Meade's staff officers, wrote that Meade showed
"extraordinary moral courage" by sustaining Warren's decision
not to attack. Meade himself felt that there would be a "great
howl" in Washington at his perceived failure.[6] To his troops,
though, Meade was a father, a caring officer who would not sacrifice them just for the sake of politicians in the capital.

Once back around Culpeper, the army built winter camps
and hunkered down until better weather appeared in the spring
of 1864. Meade established his headquarters on a knoll east of
Fleetwood Hill near Brandy Station. Cavalry covered the arc
formed by the infantry corps and their camps.

The winter remained generally quiet. Meade went to Washington late in December for a conference with Lincoln about the
problems with drafted men and substitutes, some of whom were
criminals and were being shot for various offenses. Lincoln failed
to see the wisdom in executing the worst offenders, so he and
Meade agreed on a more lenient policy—incarceration rather
than death. Margaret came down from Philadelphia and both
Meades attended a New Year's Day White House social gather-
ing hosted by the President. Meade went home on leave in mid-
January, caught a cold and came down with pneumonia,
necessitating an extended stay at home to recuperate.

On March 4, 1864, Meade went to Washington to talk with
officials about his proposed reorganization of the Army of the

Potomac. Upon arriving in the capital, the general was "greatly surprised to find the whole town talking of certain grave charges of Generals Sickles and Doubleday."[7] Indeed, ever since Gettysburg, Meade had been the target of criticism, both from the President and discontented generals. The Joint Congressional Committee on the Conduct of the War, which had been formed early in the war to oversee military and civil conduct had begun to call witnesses in February 1864 to speak to the committee about Meade's handling of the army.

Chaired by Michigan Senator Chandler, whom Meade had infuriated in 1861 by refusing to take an oath of allegiance, the committee was interested in learning more about Meade's generalship. Its first witness was Dan Sickles, who told the committee that Meade had contemplated a retreat from Gettysburg and that only the opening of the battle on his front prevented such a disastrous move. Furthermore, Sickles declared that Meade had not issued any orders to him and that removing Hooker on the eve of a great battle was a major error. General Doubleday came next to see the committee. He told them that he had been removed from command of the First Corps because Meade wanted to place his friends in positions of power, and that any anti-McClellan man did not stand a chance in that army. Brig. Gen. Albion P. Howe, a Sixth Corps division commander, chronicled Meade's inability to make decisions, his slow pursuit of Lee in July 1863, and the retreat in October 1863.

After hearing from these three generals, Chandler, accompanied by Ohio Senator Ben Wade, went to see Lincoln and demanded that he remove Meade and reinstate Hooker. Thus, when Meade came to Washington, he was called before the committee on March 5, and proceeded to defend his actions at length. The general then visited Secretary Stanton, who told Meade that the committee wanted to replace him with Hooker, but they would not succeed. Still, Meade felt that his reputation would suffer.

Over the next several weeks, a number of other officers were called upon to testify about Meade's generalship. Generals Pleasonton and Birney gave some damaging testimony about the July 2 council of war at Gettysburg and the dilatory pursuit afterward. Butterfield, serving in Tennessee with Hooker, was smuggled into the capital against orders so he could appear before the committee and further blacken Meade's reputation. Generals Warren, Gibbon, Hunt, Seth Williams, and Hancock all lined up behind Meade and told the committee that Meade was a good commander who never contemplated a retreat from Gettysburg. Meade himself appeared before the committee on two more occasions to add documents and testimony to his initial statements. In the end, the committee's 1865 report deprecated Meade because of the wasted opportunities to attack Lee during the Gettysburg Campaign and the perceived failures at Bristoe Station and Mine Run. The committee found that Pleasonton, not Meade, was the general who decided the battle would be fought at Gettysburg because Pleasonton had sent Buford's division to that town.

During the midst of the committee investigations, on March 12, 1864, an anonymous letter signed "Historicus" appeared in the influential *New York Herald.* The author, an eyewitness of Gettysburg, repeated the Sickles story so that the public could judge for itself how the battle was won and how the Army of Northern Virginia escaped afterward. Meade was especially stung by this slanderous article. He wrote an angry letter to the War Department and asked for an investigation, citing his belief that Sickles was either the author or had dictated it to a supporter. Halleck, although sympathizing with Meade's anguish, advised Meade to ignore the article because of Sickles's ability to color the press. However, other officers rallied to Meade's defense and attacked the Historicus article with letters of their own. Historicus took delight in writing a second article to answer his critics.

Although the committee failed to have Hooker reinstated to command, the voluminous testimony and related newspaper articles served to damage Meade's reputation at the time and furthermore provided subsequent uncritical historians of the battle with grist for writing their own inaccurate versions of Gettysburg. The committee hearings were only the first words in a bitter feud that would erupt much later between supporters of Meade and Sickles over the conduct of the battle of Gettysburg. The feud eventually included many prominent generals, staff officers, and regimental commanders, each of whom wrote his own account of the battle. Taken together, this mass of often vituperative literature has clogged up the true story of Gettysburg and has accorded Sickles glory he never deserved. Meade's reputation suffered even at the time, but in the end, he retained command of the Army of the Potomac.

During the committee hearings, Grant was named lieutenant general on February 26 and placed in command of all Federal armies. Meade certainly had heard the rumors swirling around that Grant would be the new army head. If so, opined Meade, he would probably want to appoint his own man as commander of the Army of the Potomac. Indeed, Grant had earlier thought that either Gen. William T. Sherman or Maj. Gen. William F. "Baldy" Smith might make a good commander. Having his own man in the East would ensure cooperation with movements west of the Appalachians. Grant's original strategy for 1864 called for simultaneous advances by all Union armies to put pressure on the Confederacy and prevent a repetition of Longstreet's detachment to Bragg. The main thrusts would be on Atlanta and Mobile, with a holding strategy in Virginia to prevent Lee from sending troops elsewhere.

When Grant traveled to Washington in March 1864, he intended to return to the West and supervise the Federal armies from that vantage point. However, his visit to Washington and the Army of the Potomac convinced him that he must remain in Virginia and allow Sherman to command the West. When Grant met Meade at Brandy Station on March 10, Meade quickly offered to step aside if the new general in chief wished to replace him. Thrown on the defensive, Grant dismissed Meade's offer and told him that he would remain in charge of the army he knew so well. Grant had become aware of the political squabbling over who would be the new commander of the Army of the Potomac, a scenario fueled by the ongoing committee hearings. This, plus the army's past history of being pulled by strings attached to the capital, influenced Grant to remain in Virginia and attempt to keep the Army as free as possible from outside sniping.

Meade himself was impressed with Grant when they first met. "I was very much pleased with Grant," he wrote to Margaret. "In the views he expressed to me he showed much more capacity and character than I had expected."[8] Ever the aristocrat, Meade may have looked down on Grant the plebian. But the Pennsylvanian, Grant's senior by seven years, also sensed that they could get along and provide mutual support. Meade thought he might now be a more effective commander once Washington's influence was minimized. However, he also prophetically warned Margaret that his own fame would suffer as a result. But Meade recognized Grant's drive and determination, preferring this attitude over Halleck's cautiousness.

Some things would never change, however. When Grant returned to Virginia later in March, he wanted to make his headquarters with the army rather than remain in Washington with the politicians. When Grant asked Meade to suggest a location, Meade recommended either Culpeper or Warrenton, but preferred Culpeper because it would place Grant closer to him. Ironically, when Grant did locate at Culpeper, the newspapers insisted that this location symbolized the new commander because Culpeper was six miles closer to Lee than Meade's own headquarters.

Chapter 7

The 1864 Campaign

I N FEBRUARY 1864, just as Meade was returning to headquarters after recovering from pneumonia, he and Secretary of War Stanton got into a dispute over reorganization of the Army of the Potomac. Stanton was in favor of disbanding the First and Third Corps, both of which had suffered heavy losses at Gettysburg, and merging them into the Second, Fifth, and Sixth. Generals French and Newton would thus be relieved, as would Sedgwick of the Sixth, whom Stanton disliked. General Sykes of the Fifth would be replaced by Warren, with Hancock resuming command of the Second Corps. Meade liked Sedgwick and fought hard to keep him in command of his corps. But the general did not fight hard to keep Pleasonton, particularly in light of the cavalry commander's testimony to the Committee on the Conduct of the War.

The reorganization order was issued in March. Meade tempered the order by allowing the former First and Third Corps divisions to retain their original corps badges. The remaining corps—Second, Fifth, and Sixth—were each increased to four divisions. Grant brought in one of his own men, Maj. Gen.

Philip Sheridan, as the new chief of the Army's Cavalry Corps. Gone also with Pleasonton was Third Division commander Brig. Gen. Judson Kilpatrick, whose failed raid on Richmond in February had created a tempest after it was alleged that documents found on the body of slain Union Col. Ulric Dahlgren called for the murder of Jefferson Davis and other high-ranking Confederate officials. Kilpatrick had gone over Meade's head directly to the President with plans for the raid. Meade wasn't convinced that it would work, and Sedgwick, who commanded the army while Meade was home on leave, severely criticized the operation in his official report.

Meanwhile, Grant had returned to Virginia and made his headquarters at Culpeper as suggested by Meade. On April 9, Grant sent Meade general instructions for the coming spring campaign. "Lee's army will be your objective point. Wherever Lee goes, there you will go also."[1] Grant fully intended to allow Meade tactical control of the army while he acted merely as an observer. Since he was general in chief, Grant needed the freedom to respond quickly to any emergency or problem on any of the active military fronts. Thus, he wanted to keep Meade in command and allow him to command the army he knew so well.

But problems between the two generals' staffs soon exacerbated an awkward command situation. Colonel Lyman of Meade's staff succinctly outlined the major problem when he wrote that Grant "has several very sensible officers on his Staff, and several very foolish ones, who talked and laughed flippantly about Lee and his army."[2] Lyman, like many other observers of the time, saw clearly that the repeated defeats suffered by the Army of the Potomac had resulted in a haughty attitude among some of the western officers, who believed that the Army and its commanders would have done better if Grant had been in charge all along. What they didn't realize, opined Lyman, was that Lee was a much better opponent than the Southern generals out west.

Assistant Secretary of War Charles A. Dana, who liked Grant and had spent months singing the general's praises in Washington, had informed Grant as early as December 21 that according to his conversations with officials in Washington regarding the Army of the Potomac, "nothing is to be hoped under its present commander." Indeed, Dana did not show any respect to Meade at all. In his postwar recollections, he penned a picture of Meade that is so far removed from the truth as to be absurd. "He is totally lacking in cordiality toward those with whom he has business, and in consequence was generally disliked by his subordinates," wrote Dana. Meade only got along with Grant because Meade "had the first virtue of a soldier—that is, obedience to orders." Meade couldn't win the war because he lacked Grant's "moral authority." "As soon as Meade had a commander over him he was all right, but when he himself was the commander he began to hesitate." Meade had the habit of promoting engineers to command positions, and, added Dana, everyone knew that engineers didn't fight, except Andrew A. Humphreys, who was an exception to the rule.[3]

Grant himself recognized Meade's ability and respected his knowledge of the Army of the Potomac. On May 13, in the midst of the operations at Spotsylvania, Grant wrote to Secretary of War Stanton regarding some promotions earned by some of the officers in the Army during the fighting thus far. Of Meade, Grant wrote: "General Meade has more than met my most sanguine expectations. He and Sherman are the fittest officers for large commands I have come in contact with. If their services can be rewarded by promotion to the rank of Maj. Gen. in the regular army the honor would be worthily bestowed and I would feel personally gratified."[4]

The 1864 operations, however, were far from smooth because of Grant's presence with the Army of the Potomac. Although he envisioned allowing Meade to control his army, as the campaign wore on, Grant, with increasing frequency, issued specific orders to Meade, who became little more than an executive officer. In fact, some historians have compared Meade's role in this campaign to Grant's in May 1862, when Halleck took charge of the armies operating against Corinth, Mississippi, and allowed

Grant little control over anything. By May 19, Meade could only agree with a recent description of the chain of command by a noted magazine editor, "directed by Grant, commanded by Meade, and led by Hancock, Sedgwick and Warren."[5] But Grant's presence would also shift blame away from Meade and on to Grant for the heavy casualties that were to be incurred.

The campaign started off smoothly enough. The Army of the Potomac broke camp on May 3 and began to edge toward the Rapidan River. Grant's plan in general paralleled Meade's wish in the fall of 1863 to edge around Lee's right flank and rely on Fredericksburg, and later the eastern Virginia rivers, for supply. The army would cross the Rapidan and quickly march through the dense forest called The Wilderness into open terrain. If Lee stood and fought, he would be outnumbered about two to one. In addition to the Army of the Potomac's three corps, Burnside's Ninth Corps was back in Virginia, acting as an independent command because Burnside was senior to Meade as a major general. Maj. Gen. Benjamin F. Butler and his Army of the James would also pressure Richmond, while Maj. Gen. Franz Sigel, operating in the Shenandoah Valley, would pin down Confederate troops there. If Lee retreated to the Richmond defenses, declared Grant, then it was only a matter of time before Union victory was certain.

Once across the Rapidan on May 4, the Union army encountered Confederate pickets, who spread the word that the Yankees were coming. Ewell's corps sidled to the right to confront the advancing enemy columns. On the morning of May 5, Meade asked Warren to ascertain what was on his front before the army continued its march out of The Wilderness. Warren reported that his cavalry pickets were being driven back and that his infantry skirmishers were engaged with the advancing enemy.

Meade quickly issued orders for Warren to deploy his corps and attack. Sedgwick received orders to send up a division, and Hancock was ordered to halt his advance until the situation became clearer. Charles Griffin, in command of the lead division, slammed into Ewell's troops and drove them back, but then had to retreat when supports failed to reinforce his attack. Griffin rode back and found Meade's headquarters, dismounted, and angrily cussed out both Warren and Brig. Gen. Horatio G. Wright for not supporting his troops. After Griffin stormed back to his division, General Grant, taken aback by Griffin's tone, asked Meade, "Who is this General Gregg? Why don't you arrest him?"

Meade, seemingly angry at Grant and his chief of staff, Gen. John A. Rawlins, who had suggested that Griffin ought to be arrested, merely replied that "It's not Gregg but Griffin. And it's only his way of talking."[6]

The resulting battle of The Wilderness of May 5–6 was a terrible struggle in the woods, where poor visibility at times precluded any effective command and control by officers on both sides. Evidence of the divided command became clear when Burnside failed to arrive on time, the result of sloppy staff work on Grant's part. The two armies remained in position on May 7, with Grant deciding to move the army to the left and attempt to outflank Lee.

Meade and his staff, attempting to move the Fifth Corps, found that the road was blocked after dark on May 7. Eventually, after getting lost while trying to avoid one of the many forest fires ignited by the fighting, Meade reached Todd's Tavern around midnight. There he found David Gregg's cavalry division in bivouac. Gregg's veterans had chased enemy cavalry toward Spotsylvania, but had no further orders. In Sheridan's absence, Meade ordered Gen. Wesley Merritt to use his brigade to clear the way for Warren's men while Gregg would deploy to protect the army's flank. Meade sent notice to Sheridan of his orders and waited for daylight.

The Army of the Potomac lost the race to Spotsylvania, with Confederate infantry from Anderson's First Corps getting to the crossroads just ahead of the Yankees. Once the result was known, Meade and Sheridan got into a heated argument after Meade accused Sheridan of disobeying orders by failing to keep the road open for the infantry. Although Meade quickly apologized once he discovered that Sheridan indeed had not received any orders, the two men with short tempers continued to spar. Finally, Sheridan snapped that if he was allowed, his men could whip Stuart, but since the army commander issued orders without consulting his cavalry chief, Sheridan declared that Meade could lead the mounted men himself and Sheridan would not issue any more orders to the corps.

Incensed, Meade stalked off to find Grant and report Sheridan's insubordination. But Meade also related to Grant what Sheridan had said about going off to find Stuart. Grant replied that Sheridan could go ahead and attack the Southern cavalry. That afternoon, acting on Grant's instructions, Meade authorized Sheridan to take two divisions and operate against the Confederate cavalry, leaving only Gregg's division to patrol the army's flanks.

The fighting at Spotsylvania occupied the Army of the Potomac from May 8–19. During those twelve days, Union casualties approached 18,000, which with the 17,666 suffered in The Wilderness, meant that the army had lost perhaps one-third of its men. The Confederates also suffered severely with at least 18,000 casualties in the two battles. By the end of the battle, Meade had been reduced to the status of a second in command as Grant began to interfere more and more with tactical orders that he allowed Meade to carry out. Meade was thus placed in the same innocuous position as Grant had been in May 1862—present but unable to function as effectively as he might have without Grant's presence. Several of Grant's staff officers wanted the general to relieve Meade from command and lead the army himself to streamline the chain of command. But Grant would not do so. He considered Meade an able commander and told his staff that he needed to concentrate on the entire war, not just the fighting in Virginia. Meade relieved him of worrying about details, and Meade also knew his army and which officers could be relied upon.

During the fighting at Spotsylvania, General Sedgwick was killed by a sharpshooter on May 9; General Wright succeeded to

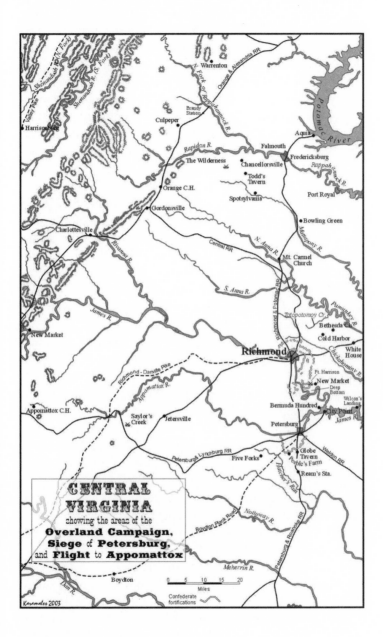

CENTRAL VIRGINIA
showing the areas of the
Overland Campaign,
Siege of **Petersburg,**
and **Flight** to **Appomattox**

0 5 10 15 20
Miles

Confederate
fortifications

Karamales 2003

Sixth Corps command. On May 11, realizing that the army probably had too many cannon, Grant suggested to Meade that the Artillery Reserve be sent back to Washington. Wooded terrain hampered its effectiveness and wasted supplies. Meade, acting on a complaint from General Hunt, ignored Grant's suggestion. Five days later, Grant directly ordered Meade to carry out his instructions. General Hunt came up with an alternative plan, reducing the batteries to four guns each and distributing the reserve batteries among the three corps. Grant approved this change, which was announced on May 17.

Following the carnage at Spotsylvania, Grant ordered another flank move and the army maneuvered south to the North Anna River. Lee retreated behind this stream and Grant followed, the army crossing at two points, leaving each flank dangerously isolated from the other. Meade's temper flared again on May 24. Both generals had halted and were resting with their staffs at Mount Carmel Church when a dispatch arrived for Grant from Sherman. Assistant Secretary of War Dana decided to read this dispatch aloud. In essence, Sherman remarked that his troops were advancing steadily and doing well. If Grant could only inspire the Army of the Potomac, the war would soon be over.

Colonel Lyman later recalled that "the eyes of Major-General George Gordon Meade stood out about one inch as he said, in a voice like cutting an iron bar with a handsaw: 'Sir! I consider that despatch [*sic*] an insult to the army I command and to me personally. The Army of the Potomac does not require General Grant's inspiration or anybody else's inspiration to make it fight!'" Meade remained angry all day and into that night. At supper, he spoke of the Western army as an "armed rabble," recalled Lyman. No one seems to have recorded Grant's reaction to Dana's acerbic wit and Meade's retort.[7]

Grant expanded Meade's authority the next day by assigning the Ninth Corps to the Army of the Potomac. Burnside agreed to serve under Meade's command even though he was the senior general, and Grant hoped to streamline the army's staff work by merging the independent Ninth Corps with the main army.

Maj. Gen. George Gordon Meade took command of the Army of the Potomac three days before it clashed with Robert E. Lee's Army of Northern Virginia at Gettysburg. Despite leading Union forces to victory in one of history's most famous battles and commanding the Army of the Potomac for the remainder of the Civil War, Meade was dogged by controversies that sullied his reputation for years afterward.
National Archives

Maj. Gen. Daniel E. Sickles (center, seated) endangered the Union forces at Gettysburg when, in an ill-conceived interpretation of his orders, he advanced his men beyond the established Union line, exposing his flanks. Soon after being reprimanded by Meade, Sickles was hit by a cannonball that would take his leg. Despite the relatively mild treatment he received from his commander, Sickles spent his convalescence, and indeed the rest of his life, defending his actions at Gettysburg and disparaging Meade.
National Archives

Maj. Gen. Daniel Butterfield aided Daniel Sickles in his post-Gettysburg effort to destroy Meade's reputation before Congress's Committee on the Conduct of the War.
National Archives

Maj. Gen. George G. Meade's headquarters during the Battle of Gettysburg was at the Leister farm on Cemetery Ridge. The farmhouse was subjected to Confederate artillery fire that overshot the Union battle lines during the bombardment that preceded Pickett's Charge on July 3, 1863. A solid cannon shot narrowly missed Meade as he stood in the doorway.
Library of Congress

In 1864, the U.S. Congress appointed Ulysses S. Grant the first lieutenant general in the American military since George Washington. Though general in chief of all Union armies, Grant made his headquarters with the Army of the Potomac. While Meade retained his command, Grant's presence soon overshadowed Meade's leadership, a fact emphasized by the Civil War–era press and subsequent histories of the conflict.
National Archives

This council of war at Massaponax Church, Virginia, in May 1864, was attended by Lt. Gen. Ulysses S. Grant, Maj. Gen. George G. Meade, Assistant Secretary of War Charles A. Dana, and numerous staff officers. Grant (at left, leaning over bench) examines a map held by Meade.
Library of Congress

Maj. Gen. George G. Meade (seated, fifth from left) and his staff in the vicinity of Washington, D.C., June 1865. *Library of Congress*

Fighting along the North Anna took place May 23–25, with no clear advantage to the Yankees. Therefore, Grant withdrew the army to the north bank and ordered yet another flank march toward the east. Lee paralleled Meade's troops, and a series of engagements at Totopotomoy Creek, Bethesda Church, and the Pamunkey River, took place May 28–31. Grant then ordered a movement toward the Chickahominy River, frustrated that Lee would not fight out in the open.

Another movement brought the armies to the crossroads of Cold Harbor, near the old Gaines's Mill battlefield. Yankee cavalry seized the road junction on May 31 as the infantry followed. Confederate attempts to recapture the crossroads were rebuffed on the first of June. Meade suggested further attacks to catch the enemy off balance, to which Grant assented. However, the gains made that day resulted in more than 2,200 casualties. Grant then decided to attack again on June 2 before the enemy could entrench firmly all along their line. But Hancock's corps was late in arriving and the general postponed the attack until early on June 3. By that time, Lee's troops had entrenched and bloodily repelled the Yankee attacks, inflicting more than 4,600 casualties.

Two days later, Meade composed a thoughtful letter to Margaret. The general now could profess a clear conscience over the attacks that did not take place at Williamsport and Mine Run. In every instance of an attack on fortifications, except at Spotsylvania, "which was a surprise discreditable to the enemy," wrote Meade, the attackers have been repulsed. Grant now realized that "Virginia and Lee's army is not Tennessee and Bragg's army. Whether the people will ever realize this fact remains to be seen."[8]

Even as the fighting at Cold Harbor erupted, the *Philadelphia Inquirer* printed a story by Edward Cropsey about the campaign thus far. Generally, the article was favorable to Meade. However, the general was puzzled about one vague section of Cropsey's tale. "History will record, but newspapers cannot, that on one eventful night during the present campaign, Grant's presence saved the army and the nation too; not that Gen. Meade was on the point of committing a blunder unwittingly, but his devotion to his country made him loth to risk her last army on what he deemed a chance. Grant assumed the responsibility, and we are still 'On to Richmond'."[9]

Meade soon called Cropsey to his headquarters and demanded to know what this part of the article was all about. The reporter replied that he heard that Meade urged Grant to withdraw across the Rapidan after The Wilderness fighting had ended, but Grant firmly resisted such an idea and instead turned the army south. When asked where he got this information, Cropsey said it was the talk of the camp. Meade exploded with rage. Talk of the camp indeed! The general wrote that he called the tale "a base and wicked lie," and promised the reporter that he would make an example of him.[10]

On June 7, Meade issued an order expelling Cropsey from the camp. Brig. Gen. Marsena R. Patrick, Meade's provost general, was only too happy to comply with the general's wishes. Cropsey was seized, mounted backward on a mule, collared with a sign painted with "libeler of the press," and paraded through camp before being escorted beyond the lines. Meade said Grant was present when he wrote the order and fully approved it. But Meade's own short fuse proved to be detrimental this time. Other reporters, angry over Cropsey's treatment, banded together and decided not to mention Meade's name in their newspapers for at least six months, unless Meade suffered a defeat. His name was even omitted when printing dispatches from Army headquarters.

Still seething over the Cropsey incident, Meade's temper was further aggravated the next day. Grant was planning his movement across the James River and wanted to throw up some earthworks to protect the army as it moved. The general in chief sent one of his own staff officers to point out the line to be constructed. To Meade, this was a slight on Grant's part. Generals Hancock and Gibbon visited Meade that night to find the general still upset over the fact that his opinion had not been courted when Grant issued his instructions. Gibbon thought that Meade was simply suffering from the strain now evident throughout the Army. Still, Gibbon realized that Meade was "a man of a peculiarly excitable disposition and his sensibility was such that he very quickly felt any lack of deference to himself or respect for his position."[11] One wonders if these two incidents contributed to the command breakdown a week later at Petersburg.

Chapter 8

Petersburg

Having been rebuffed at Cold Harbor, Grant decided to send the Army of the Potomac across the James River to attack Petersburg. Located twenty miles south of Richmond, Petersburg was a vital rail center and supply point, which, if seized, would force Lee to evacuate Richmond. Accordingly, Warren and his Fifth Corps, accompanied by a cavalry division, moved to the left of the line, forcing Lee to stretch his troops to cover a supposed Federal attack toward Richmond. In the meantime, engineer officers moved to the James to locate proper crossing points. Meade prepared all the materials for building pontoon bridges and had the engineers ready once the plan was finalized. By midnight on June 15, engineers working from both banks of the James built a 2,100-foot bridge across the river at Wilcox's Landing.

Even as the engineers worked, Hancock's Second Corps began crossing by steamers a short distance above the bridge site. By 3:30 A.M. on June 15, the entire Second Corps was across the river and ready to march. Meanwhile, Baldy Smith's Eighteenth Corps, which had marched from Cold Harbor to White House, there boarding ships for a quick trip down the York River and up the James, had landed and advanced on Petersburg. Grant had ordered Butler to launch Smith's corps against Petersburg as soon as it arrived at Bermuda Hundred, and also to supply Hancock's divisions with rations after the Second Corps crossed the river. Hancock would then march to support Butler. Once the rest of the Army of the Potomac was across, it would move to reinforce Smith and Hancock.

At least this is what Grant envisioned. But sloppy staff work negated any surprise that Grant's swift movement from Cold Harbor to Petersburg produced. Butler failed to specifically order Smith to attack Petersburg with his entire corps. Instead, Smith was overly cautious when his troops easily penetrated the lightly held outer defenses of Petersburg. Completely in the dark, Lee had not yet realized that Grant's entire force was moving south of the James. Meade was equally in the dark because Grant failed to communicate his intentions and plans at first. Meade thus remained in the rear, supervising the pontoon bridge construction and making sure that the army was kept on the move and headed across the river as planned.

The resulting initial attacks on Petersburg failed to produce the decisive capture that Grant had planned. Smith was fooled by Gen. P. G. T. Beauregard's small number of troops. Grant's move had surprised and fixed Lee in place north of the James, but Smith wasted a valuable opportunity and plodded forward cautiously. Meade, receiving word of the initial fighting, seemed to be surprised but quickly realized that more troops would be needed. He turned aside much of the artillery to enable Burnside's corps to cross the James, even while he ordered Warren to begin sending his troops across by steamer to quicken the transfer across the river. Sheridan and two cavalry divisions were absent on a raid, leaving Brig. Gen. James H. Wilson's Third Division to guard the army trains as they prepared to follow the infantry. Thus, the attacks on Petersburg were not given the benefit of prior cavalry reconnaissance.

Meade remained behind to supervise the army's crossing of

the James as June 16 dawned. Grant and his staff rode off to the front right after breakfast to survey the situation. Meade met Grant returning from his ride later that day. Grant informed Meade that Smith had taken some very strong earthworks and Hancock was also advancing. "If it is a possible thing," the general in chief ordered, "I want an attack made at six o'clock this evening."[1]

Meade and his staff continued on and found Hancock, whose artillery was firing at distant enemy fortifications. Meade, Humphreys, and Brig. Gen. Francis C. Barlow rode ahead to survey the situation and could see the church spires of Petersburg some distance ahead. Hancock's men soon went forward and gained more ground as Capt. Horace Porter of Grant's staff arrived to ask that the assault be pushed to draw off enemy attention from Bermuda Hundred, which was under pressure from enemy attacks. After losing 2,500 men, the Army of the Potomac's June 16 attacks ended as darkness fell.

Warren and the Fifth Corps began to arrive during the night and morning of June 17, as did Burnside and the entire Ninth Corps. A Sixth Corps division followed. Meade kept extending the army's front as Burnside attacked, taking some more entrenchments and prisoners. But Warren massed his troops and then reconnoitered, failing to make any serious assaults at all during the seventeenth. Hancock's old Gettysburg wound opened during the day and he had to turn command of his corps over to Gen. Birney.

The morning of the eighteenth showed that Meade was by then in an ugly mood. Meade had expected the Fifth Corps to attack promptly at 4:00 A.M. to support Burnside's further assaults. During the night, the Confederates had withdrawn from their outer works into a new line constructed closer to the city. As a result, the Yankee advance slowed down as the troops groped forward to locate the enemy. Meade became upset over Warren's cautiousness on the left of the line and finally ordered that an attack be made by noon. But only the right flank stirred and gained some minor successes. Finally, at 2:00 P.M., a disgusted Meade ordered each corps commander to attack on his own responsibility without waiting for the others. The result was a series of bloody repulses all along the line as Beauregard was reinforced by the Army of Northern Virginia. Lee had finally realized that the entire Yankee army was across the James. When darkness fell, Meade ordered the troops to remain in position and entrench.

Captain Porter, sent by Grant to assist Meade if needed, described Meade that day: "He showed himself the personification of earnest, vigorous action in rousing his subordinate commanders to superior exertions. Even his fits of anger and his resort to intemperate language stood him at times in good stead in spurring on every one upon that active field. He sent ringing dispatches to all points of the line, and paced up and down upon the field in his nervous, restless manner, as he watched the progress of the operations and made running comments on the actions of his subordinates. His aquiline nose and piercing eyes gave him something of an eagle's look, and added to the interest of his personality. He had much to try him upon this occasion, and if he was severe in his reprimands and showed faults of temper, he certainly displayed no faults as a commander."[2]

In his first real chance since The Wilderness to command the army in combat, Meade failed. The general was simply unable to prompt his corps commanders into launching coordinated assaults against the outnumbered defenders. Meade allowed Warren's vacillation to overrule his initial desire to launch the Fifth Corps into a quick attack. Without cavalry to protect the army's left flank, both Meade and Warren worried about being outflanked. As a result, the Fifth Corps was unable to support Hancock's and Burnside's attacks.

Meade himself was beginning to doubt the army's ability to avoid a prolonged siege of Petersburg. When he wrote to Margaret on the evening of June 17, the general candidly informed her that such would probably be the case. After the failure of the June 18 attacks, siege operations followed.

Most of the blame for the failure of the June 15–18 attacks rests equally with Grant and Meade. Grant remained detached from the tactical operations and provided no support for his beleaguered lieutenant, who could not get much cooperation from his corps commanders. General Gibbon, whose division took part in these attacks, believed that the Army of the Potomac was simply exhausted and could do no better. The constant marching and fighting since May 5 had taken its toll. In Gibbon's division, the casualty rate through May 31 was 47 percent; by July 31, he had used seventeen different brigade commanders, nine of whom were killed. Gibbon also saw forty of his regimental commanders killed or wounded, and many of his best men were laid hors de combat. Considering handicaps such as these, the army had done quite well.

Meade next commanded the strike against the Weldon Railroad on June 22–23. Grant ordered the foray, but left it up to Meade to choose the troops and conduct the operation. As with the botched attacks on Petersburg, Meade again had problems with his subordinates. The Second Corps, still led by General Birney, did not acquit itself very favorably. Wright, leading the Sixth Corps, delayed when he noticed enemy troops moving across his front on June 23. Informed of this, Meade ordered Wright to take the initiative and attack if Southern troops threatened his line, unless such a course would endanger his own flank. Throughout the afternoon, Meade sent at least two more attack orders to Wright, but the general dallied and darkness ended any chance for a successful operation. In reporting the day's events to Grant, a frustrated Meade ended with "I think you had better come up tomorrow if convenient."[3]

The June 22–23 operation illustrates Grant's and Meade's roles in the Petersburg operations for the rest of the siege. Grant, based in his headquarters at City Point, initiated all the expeditions and left Meade to command the Army of the Potomac with little interference on his part. On at least one occasion, Grant heeded Meade's advice about projected movements.

Grant wished to take part of the Army of the Potomac, cut loose from the siege lines, and intersect Lee's supplies by moving north of the Appomattox River. Meade counseled against this idea by telling Grant that too many things could go wrong, especially a lack of supplies. This could force the army to take the initiative against Lee's entrenched troops without proper communications. Grant listened to Meade and abandoned this plan.

Throughout the Petersburg operations, Meade's relations with his subordinates were stormy at times. The general became increasingly displeased with Warren's performance as a corps commander. On June 21, Meade addressed a letter to Rawlins, Grant's chief of staff, in which he outlined Warren's problems. "The defect in Genl. Warren consists in too great reliance on his own judgment, and in an apparent impossibility on his part to yield his judgment so as to promptly execute orders, where these orders should happen not to receive his sanction or be in accordance with his views."

Meade reviewed Warren's decision not to attack at Mine Run and the subsequent wasted time when he sent to headquarters for additional instructions. On May 12, Warren seemed unwilling or unable to direct the Fifth Corps against Lee's left flank at Spotsylvania. At that time, Grant wanted to relieve Warren but Meade interceded and instead sent Humphreys to assist Warren. Finally, on June 18, Warren again delayed and did not promptly obey Meade's order to advance to the attack. When Meade berated Warren the next day, the corps commander "exhibited so much temper and bad feeling" that Meade decided he would have Warren transferred to another command. However, Meade never sent the letter he prepared. He first showed it to Warren in a private session and then lectured Warren on his proper responsibilities.[4]

Meade normally got along well with Hancock, but had some slight problems with Gibbon for a short time. After Gibbon's division was whipped at Reams's Station in August, the general issued an order revoking the right to carry colors of the three units because of their cowardice in this engagement. Meade saw the order and thought it was a good way to help restore some unit pride, and on September 23 had the order extended to cover the entire Army of the Potomac. Gibbon was miffed at this application of his idea because it publicized his own regiments' ineptitude before the whole army.

Meade had a major feud with General Burnside because of the Crater debacle. When Col. Henry Pleasants of the Forty-eighth Pennsylvania proposed digging a tunnel under an enemy salient, then filling the end of the tunnel with gunpowder and lighting a match, Meade disapproved of the idea. His engineering training made him conclude that the tunnel was impracticable because of its length, which was too long for fresh air to reach the miners. The general also thought the terrain in the area was unfavorable for digging operations since the enemy would be able to repair a gap in the line by placing troops on the ridge behind the projected mine. Still, Meade authorized the attempt to be made, believing, apparently, that the men could be kept busy. Army headquarters provided no logistical support for the tunnel operation.

Then, when Burnside said that his Fourth Division, composed of black troops, would lead the attack, Meade vetoed the idea. Meade argued that the division was largely untested in combat, and if the attack failed, abolitionists would criticize the use of black soldiers as a forlorn hope. Meade instead told Burnside to use another division for the initial assault wave. He could not have foreseen that Burnside would authorize his three white division commanders to draw straws and that the weakest commander would get the short straw. In the meantime, Meade drew up detailed instructions for the July 30 attack that Grant pronounced as quite complete.

During the July 30 fighting, Meade remained at his headquarters to coordinate the movements of troops, replying on dispatches from the front to supply the needed information to enable him to assess the battle's development. When a dispatch meant for Burnside instead was sent to army headquarters revealing disastrous developments in the Crater, Meade blew up.

He immediately sent word to Burnside that he wanted a full report on the situation. Burnside interpreted Meade's dispatch to mean that the army commander believed that he was not telling the truth. The two generals traded barbs via messenger until Burnside rode back to Meade's headquarters and the two officers got into a shouting match with foul language. All in all, neither man conducted himself properly that day. Meade probably should have moved closer to the front line, but chose instead to remain at army headquarters where he was able to receive all dispatches as soon as they arrived. Such an action was in keeping with Meade's command style—allowing the corps commanders to run the tactical operations with a minimum of interference from him.

The resulting official inquiry into the causes of the Crater disaster earned Meade more enemies in Congress. Meade received some of the blame for the failure for his decision not to allow the black troops to lead the attack. This hurt his chances of promotion in the Regular Army. When the Middle Military Division was formed in July to streamline operations in the Shenandoah Valley, Meade hoped that he might be transferred to this command and thus escape Grant's shadow. Grant had originally nominated General Franklin for this new district, but the government refused. Grant then sought Meade, but Lincoln was opposed on the ground that if Meade was transferred from the Army of the Potomac, it might appear to the public that the general was being relieved from command, and the President did not want it to appear that way. Still, Lincoln told Grant that if Meade wished the transfer, he would be very glad to make it.

After receiving this explanation from Grant, Meade took time to write Margaret about the prospects of being transferred. "I am a little doubtful about this matter," he said. "I believe Grant is honest and would not deceive me, but I think there is something more than is acknowledged. However, as I am indifferent about the position, I am content, so long as finding any fault with me is disclaimed." When the order assigning Sheridan to the command of the division was announced, Meade asked Grant why he was not picked instead of his junior. "To which he made no remark. I really am not able to ascertain what are his real views. Sometimes I take the dark side, and think they are intentionally adverse to me, and at others I try to make myself believe that such is not his purpose."[5]

Meade was further frustrated when Grant nominated Sherman, Hancock, and Sheridan as major generals in the Regular Army, but left Meade's name off the list. Grant wanted Sherman to outrank Meade. Grant explained to an outraged Meade that he could not push his name at present (early August) because Sheridan had just suffered a repulse and the public might see Meade's name instead of Sheridan's as a censure of Sheridan. Meade remained silent until October, when he again wished to know what was blocking his promotion. He learned that there was some congressional opposition because of the Burnside imbroglio, but Grant quickly sent off some letters and the situation was finally cleared up in February 1865, when Meade was finally promoted, to rank from August 18, 1864.

The Crater failure allowed several newspaper editors to take some more shots at Meade and his officers. Earlier that summer, Grant had ordered two correspondents expelled after committing some outrageous behavior. William Swinton of the *New York Times* was caught eavesdropping on a conversation between Grant and Meade, and William Kent of the *New York Tribune* had slandered Hancock and the Second Corps. Even though Grant ordered them evicted, it was Meade who issued the specific orders and caught the fury of the press in return. The *New York Herald* predicted Meade would be relieved, while the *Times* commented on Meade's furious temper. Grant could have spoken out against such slanders on the army commander, but he never did, causing Meade to wonder whose side he was on.

As Meade fought these battles behind the scenes, the Petersburg siege dragged on. After the failure at the Crater, the Union forces remained quiet until mid-August, when Grant ordered another push to the west against the Weldon Railroad, one of three railroads feeding into Petersburg from the south. A successful thrust against this railroad would mean that two of the three would be under Federal control and thus further exacerbate Lee's supply problems. Hancock's corps went north of the James to occupy enemy attention at Deep Bottom while the Fifth Corps marched west to the Weldon, occupying the line and fending off a Southern attack at Globe Tavern on August 19. Reinforced by part of the Ninth Corps, now under the capable command of Maj. Gen. John G. Parke, Warren managed to hold on through a second day of fighting. Worried about the enemy intentions, Grant ordered Hancock to disengage and march west to help Warren.

Even though the corps was exhausted after marching all night to reach the scene, Hancock had his troops in hand and they began tearing up the track as far as Reams's Station, some fifteen miles south of Warren's position, on August 22. The destruction of the railroad continued until August 25, when a sudden enemy counterattack caught the Second Corps by surprise and captured more than 2,000 prisoners and nine cannon. Although Hancock's men were driven back, Warren remained astride the railroad behind strong fortifications. At least this thrust had resulted in the occupation of the Weldon Railroad, depriving Lee of its direct services.

The Weldon battle heralded a period of relative inactivity for the Yankees around Petersburg. Meade himself managed to get home for four days to look after his son Sergeant, who had developed tuberculosis and was wasting away from the dreaded disease. Sherman occupied Atlanta on September 2 and Sheridan won a victory at Winchester on September 19, causing Grant to launch another offensive at Lee's army.

The Army of the James moved north of its namesake river and launched an attack at New Market Heights, capturing Fort Harrison but was unable to achieve a breakthrough. On the west end of the line, the Fifth and Ninth Corps marched west and engaged enemy troops on September 30–October 1, in fighting at Peebles's farm. Although the Ninth Corps was flanked and hundreds of its men captured, Warren's men dug in and Meade spent several days supervising the construction of a new line of works to connect with Warren's gains. Upon completion, the Union line ran more than twenty miles to the Appomattox River, with a specially built military railroad able to supply the troops with the best equipment and food available.

Following Sheridan's decisive victory on October 19 at Cedar Creek, Grant authorized yet another strike against Lee's defenses. Butler moved north of the James and was fended off at the second battle of Fair Oaks, while on the other flank, Grant and Meade personally accompanied troops from the Second, Fifth, and Ninth Corps, which fought a battle known as the Boydton Plank Road on October 27–28. Bad weather limited Federal mobility. On the twenty-seventh, Grant and Meade came under fire as they reconnoitered; Confederate artillery erupted around them, killing one and wounding two of Grant's staffers. The continued heavy rain and wooded terrain limited any Federal success, so Grant called off the movement.

November 8 was the day for the 1864 presidential election. Neither Grant nor Meade voted, although Meade had to restrain a few political agents who were caught in some of the soldiers' camps supplying altered ballots that favored Democratic candidates. The Army of the Potomac favored Lincoln over McClellan by a two-to-one margin.

Later in the month, General Hancock departed the army for the last time. His old Gettysburg wound still troubled the general, who was unable to be as active as required of a corps commander, so General Humphreys, eager to return to a military command, received the Second Corps. Hancock went north to superintend the creation of a new veteran corps. Hancock and Meade were not on the best of terms when Hancock left the army in late November. The issue of depriving some of Hancock's units of colors for cowardice in battle had something to do with the coolness between the two Pennsylvanians, as did a difficult problem Hancock had with newspaper reporters who were criticizing his generalship. Meade did not intervene with the press on Hancock's behalf because of the expulsion of Swinton and Kent earlier that fall. Instead, Meade recommended that Hancock draw up formal charges against the reporters, a process that had not been completed when Hancock went north.

Meade managed to obtain a leave of absence and was able to celebrate his forty-ninth birthday and twenty-fourth wedding anniversary at home with Margaret. The time was not happy though, because his son's health was failing. Sergeant was still in danger when Meade left for the front on January 9, 1865. Meade was home again late in January when his son's health suddenly got worse. The general was exasperated because he could not remain at home while Grant was home as well. Thus, when Sergeant passed away on February 21, Grant sent Meade home for the funeral via special boat.

The year of 1864 had been a very trying time for General Meade. As Meade had predicted before the campaign began, Grant's presence with the Army of the Potomac overshadowed his contributions and management of his army. As a result, the general's short temper flared more and more as the months went by. The Edward Cropsey incident plagued Meade for months, while the fiasco at the Crater and the resulting congressional investigation hampered his promotion in the Regular Army. The heavy casualties incurred during the campaign seriously impaired the army's fighting ability, as did the turnover in unit commanders as a result. When Meade did command the strikes at Petersburg's railroads, these problems manifested themselves when his subordinates failed to act decisively in spite of Meade's prodding. Still, Grant's determined plan of operations had worn down Lee's army as well. As the spring of 1865 approached, it was all too apparent that the end of the war was in sight.

Chapter 9

The End of the Civil War

I<small>N BETWEEN</small> attending to his family in Philadelphia, Meade continued to superintend the Army of the Potomac. Following Hancock's departure and Humphreys's transfer to the Second Corps, Meade chose General Webb as his new chief of staff. A West Pointer then only twenty-four years old, Webb had risen through the ranks to Meade's chief of staff in the Fifth Corps and then to brigade command at Gettysburg.

On February 5–6, Warren and Humphreys moved to the left and fought an inconclusive engagement known as Hatcher's Run, a successful move nevertheless, resulting in a further extension of the Yankee siege lines.

In late March, Mrs. Meade and a large party of Philadelphians came to visit the army, as did the President and his wife. Grant and Meade met their visitors at City Point where they entertained their guests. Grant invited Meade to stay overnight at his headquarters before returning to the army on March 25. Thus, Meade was in the rear when Lee launched his last offensive of the war, capturing Fort Stedman and temporarily breaching the Ninth Corps line that very morning. Warned by telegraph of the fighting, Meade sent orders to Webb to assist in patching the line, but the Ninth Corps managed to repel the enemy, seizing almost 2,000 prisoners in the process. Fighting erupted elsewhere along the lines, and Meade was able to report that night a catch of some 2,700 prisoners.

Grant quickly realized that Lee's strength was ebbing and so ordered Meade and his other commanders to prepare for active campaigning to begin the last week of March rather than later. Grant planned to move again toward the left, using troops from the Army of the James (now led by General Ord) as well as Meade's Second and Fifth Corps, together with Sheridan's cavalry.

The movement began on March 27 as Ord edged toward the left. Muddy weather hampered the progress of Warren's troops, who nevertheless pushed steadily on against enemy opposition. The climax came on April 1, when Warren's infantry joined Sheridan in crushing troops led by Gen. George E. Pickett at Five Forks, thereby threatening Lee's right flank. Command and control problems surfaced during this movement, resulting in Warren being attached to Sheridan, who relieved Warren of command even as his infantry sealed the victory. After the war, Warren continually attempted to obtain justice. Finally, in 1882, a military court found that Warren should have started his men forward earlier but that he had acquitted himself well during the Five Forks battle.

Hearing of the victory, Meade issued orders for Parke and Wright to assault the Petersburg entrenchments at four o'clock the next morning. Grant counseled caution, but Meade ordered Wright to follow up his assault with his entire corps. And indeed, Wright's attack rolled over the lightly held enemy line in his front and decisively breached the Confederate line. Parke's attacks crashed into the line and suffered heavy casualties, but the Ninth Corps also managed to breach the enemy siege line by day's end. By this time, Meade was suffering from a heavy cold, but he still managed to inform Grant that the lines were now breached, with Wright taking less than fifteen minutes to crack the enemy defenses.

Lee, meanwhile, decided to evacuate Petersburg and so informed President Davis, who ordered the evacuation of Richmond as well. Thus, the ten-month siege of Petersburg ended with a decisive Federal victory against Lee's outnumbered Army of Northern Virginia. Lee was fortunate to manage to get most of his army away from the doomed cities. Meade wanted to move quickly and cut off retreating enemy troops on his left, but could not obtain cooperation from Sheridan in so doing. Meade could request Sheridan's help, but since Sheridan was not under Meade's direct command, he could not order the cavalry commander to assist his infantry divisions. As a result, Lee managed to slip away with most of his remaining soldiers. Instead of crossing the Appomattox to confront Lee, Meade was only able to suggest to Grant that some of his troops be placed under Sheridan's command to ensure better cooperation.

As a result of Federal bickering, Lee evacuated Petersburg, crossed the Appomattox, then turned west, again crossing the meandering river farther west as his men raced to get ahead of pursuing Federals who advanced south of the Appomattox. On April 3, Grant and Meade rode through Petersburg, where President Lincoln met them. The generals decided upon a plan for following Lee. Sheridan's cavalry would lead the Second, Fifth, and Sixth Corps, while Ord and Parke would advance along the Southside Railroad. Meade would accompany the main column, while Grant rode with Ord.

Meade still suffered from his cold, now accompanied by a chill, but he plainly saw that the war might come to an end should his army catch up with Lee. So he spurred Humphreys on as the troops paralleled the Appomattox until that river's course turned away to the right, or north. Humphreys, on April 4, was held up by one of Ord's divisions, and then by cavalry. Rain bogged down supply trains, so Meade ordered the men to move on without them. He slept in Humphreys's tent that night, utterly exhausted by his exertions during the day.

Acting upon information from Sheridan, Meade turned the column north toward Jetersville to intersect Lee's retreating army. Meade's orders indicated that he expected the troops to undergo some privations, but in return they would end the war successfully on April 5. However, Sheridan's cavalry again slowed the march of the infantry, allowing Lee to get ahead of the pursuing Federals. Still, Lee had to change his line of retreat toward Burkeville to avoid the oncoming Army of the Potomac.

That night, Grant, after hearing from Sheridan, met with his cavalry commander and authorized him to ride straight west in an effort to get ahead of Lee's army. Meade had earlier offered to place Wright under Sheridan's command if the diminutive Sheridan needed infantry support. However, Sheridan preferred to ride off on his own rather than cooperate with Meade. Thus, the Army of the Potomac had no cavalry to scout as it advanced.

General Humphreys located the rear guard of Lee's army and shattered it on April 6. Meanwhile, Wright continued on and struck Ewell's corps at Saylor's Creek. Aided by a flank attack by Sheridan, Wright destroyed the enemy formations and captured 8,000 prisoners, a quarter of Lee's remaining strength. Sheridan reported the day's fighting to Grant via Meade's headquarters. His dispatch indicated that his troops had done all the fighting, to which Meade remarked, "Oh! So General Wright wasn't there."[1] Sheridan received the lion's share of the press coverage, which largely focused on the horsemen and not the Army of the Potomac. Meade saw that his name was rarely mentioned, and that Humphreys's and Wright's actions were buried in other stories.

Meade sent Humphreys and Wright on against Lee's retreating army, even as Sheridan, accompanied by Griffin and the Fifth Corps, followed by Ord's Twenty-fourth Corps, circled south of the enemy in an attempt to cut them off. By nightfall on April 8, Sheridan had indeed ranged ahead of the enemy as Meade and Grant bivouacked together in a small rural farmhouse. Meade had been traveling in an ambulance and was still sick, as was his chief, who was suffering from a lingering headache.

Grant and Lee had already begun exchanging notes about a

possible surrender. After leaving Meade on the morning of April 9, 1865, Grant rode to his historic meeting with Lee in the Wilmer McLean house in the small village of Appomattox Court House. There, Lee and Grant signed surrender terms and the South's major army was no more. Meade did not accompany Grant to see Lee. Instead, he spurred his troops onward as Sheridan's artillery could be heard in the distance. Humphreys was about to send the Second Corps forward when a messenger came through the lines to arrange a truce. Meade halted the attack and the troops lounged around, waiting for more news. Finally, after hearing of Lee's surrender, Meade rode back along the line, stopping at each regiment to announce the news. "Such yelling and cheering I never heard," wrote son George to his mother.[2] General Webb happily observed the scene as men in blue wept, yelled for all they were worth, and screamed Meade's name as the general rode through the victorious army.

On Monday, April 10, Meade and his staff passed through the enemy line in search of General Lee. Seeing the general approaching on horseback, Meade bowed and removed his cap. Lee at first did not recognize Meade, having not seen him for eighteen years. His first question was, "What are you doing with all that gray in your beard?" Meade responded with "You have to answer for most of it."[3] The two generals then went into Lee's tent and spent some time discussing the siege operations at Petersburg.

Meade also found his brother-in-law, Confederate Gen. Henry A. Wise. After briefly conversing with Wise, Meade loaned him $50, and ordered that two mules and an ambulance loaded with supplies be sent back to the Wise family, still in Richmond.

Following Lee's surrender, the Army of the Potomac moved into camps around Burkeville to await further events. Bad weather dampened morale, and when newspapers began arriving in camp that gave all the laurels of the campaign to Sheridan, the troops simmered along with their commanders. Meade himself called their stories "full of falsehood and undue and exaggerated praise of certain individuals who take great pains to be on the right side of the reporters." Continued Meade, "I don't believe the truth will ever be known, and I have a great contempt for History."[4]

Lincoln's assassination certainly added more bad news as the troops awaited orders. And then Henry Halleck, banished from Washington by Grant, appeared in Richmond as head of the Army's new Department of Virginia. Halleck was thus placed over Meade's head without any warning, further angering the army commander. But finally, on May 1, Meade received orders to march the Army of the Potomac through Richmond to Washington.

On May 23, General Meade led the Second, Fifth, and Ninth Corps, two cavalry divisions, and the reserve artillery on the first day of the momentous Grand Review. The veteran soldiers marched down Pennsylvania Avenue, led by Meade astride Blacky. The general halted at the reviewing stand, where he dismounted and took his place among his family after shaking hands with General Sherman. The Western armies marched the next day, after which the troops began their mustering-out processes and headed back to their individual states for final discharge. Meade and Humphreys led a parade of Pennsylvania regiments through Philadelphia on June 10, a downpour of rain failing to disperse the crowds of onlookers.

As the war was now over, Meade was assigned to the command of the Division of the Atlantic, with headquarters in Philadelphia. While this command was organized, Meade was feted and given numerous honors for his part in the war. The Meades joined Colonel Lyman at Harvard's commencement exercises, during which the general received an honorary doctor of laws degree.

Perhaps the greatest honor Meade received took place on July 4, 1866. On that memorable day, the general participated in the official return of Pennsylvania's Civil War flags to the care of the state. The ceremony took place in Philadelphia, where a parade through the city ended at Independence Hall. A grandstand was erected to accommodate 6,000 of the thousands of spectators who thronged the parade route to catch a glimpse of the state's battle-torn banners and her famous generals, including Meade, Hancock, Gregg, Geary, Samuel W. Crawford, John R. Brooke, and James S. Negley.

General Meade was chosen to present the flag of the Eighty-second Pennsylvania to Governor Curtin in a symbolic act of returning the state's battle flags to the Governor who had presented so many of them to Pennsylvania's regiments throughout the war. Meade delivered a stirring speech, noting that "of all the honors that have been showered upon me for the humble services which it has been in my power to render to my country, none have been so grateful to me, and of none am I so proud, as being on this occasion the representative of these hardy and noble men who stand before you."[5]

Chapter 10

Postwar Years

ASSIGNMENT TO the command of the Military Division of the Atlantic, with headquarters in Philadelphia, was a godsend for Meade, worn out from four years of military service. He was able to be home with his family while attending to his official duties. Since his command included the states of Virginia, North Carolina, and South Carolina, one of Meade's principal duties included a lengthy tour of inspection of the three former Confederate states. His written report of the conditions then existing in the Southern states showed that he opposed the use of black troops to maintain law and order. To Meade, this just exacerbated the already bitter sentiments expressed by many defeated Southerners, but the general had to tread carefully to avoid offending abolitionist opinion.

Meade also was aware of the growing Fenian menace along the Canadian border. Fenians were Americans of Irish descent who favored an invasion of Canada to hold that country hostage until England would free Ireland from her control. Headed by former Union Gen. Thomas W. Sweeny, thousands of Fenians, many of them Union veterans, began moving north toward the border as their agents bought weapons and ammunition from overstocked Federal arsenals.

In the spring of 1866, Fenian soldiers landed on a Canadian island and destroyed some public property there. Grant, still in command of the U.S. Army, ordered Meade to the border to disrupt any more Fenian depredations. Meade went to Eastport, Maine, and managed to prevent additional Fenian incursions into Canada.

In May, Sweeny sent a column of troops across the Niagara River into Canada. Local militia units were defeated by the Irish American veterans before Meade arrived in Buffalo. Regular Canadian troops drove the Fenians back across the river, where Meade's troops intercepted them. The general forbade any Fenian meetings, placed guards all along the Niagara, and urged the Fenian soldiers to go home to avoid prosecution. Meade even offered government payment of their travel expenses if they would just go home. The general's presence so disrupted Fenian plans that the Buffalo area quieted down very quickly. Meade and his troops followed Sweeny as he traveled to St. Albans, Vermont, where Sweeny was arrested in June and held for trial. Meade's actions quelled any future Fenian threat, allowing him to return to Philadelphia later in June.

In August, the Federal military departments were changed and Meade found himself in command of the Department of the East, with headquarters remaining in Philadelphia. Affairs remained quiet in Meade's district, but in December 1867, President Andrew Johnson appointed the general to the command of the Third Military District, embracing the states of Georgia, Alabama, and Florida, with headquarters in Atlanta. Local newspapers at first hailed Meade's appointment, declaring him to be more like a Virginia gentleman than a Northern tyrant such as General Pope, Meade's predecessor.

But opinion quickly turned against Meade when he followed Pope's course in removing some Georgia officials who opposed the Reconstruction government. Still, Meade was able to befriend former Confederate officers who vouched for his evenhanded approach to problems, thus winning back some support for his administration. Meade's chief accomplishment was to assist in paving the way for each state to elect a new government so it could be readmitted to the Union. Meade thereupon allowed, as much as possible, the new civil governments to function without military intervention.

In August 1868, the departments were again changed and Meade received command of the Department of the South, which included the three former states under his command plus the Carolinas. Meade continued in this position until March 1869, when he was reassigned to the Military Division of the Atlantic. One of the general's reports indicated his problems as a Reconstruction commander: "Notwithstanding the utmost effort on my part . . . I found myself the subject of virulent abuse, my motives impugned, and every imaginable mode of attack resorted to that malice and partisan malignity could devise. Determined from the first to ignore all partisan considerations . . . I encountered . . . the animosity of both sides, without having the benefit of the sympathy of either."[1]

Grant won the presidential election of 1868. He took office on March 4, 1869. One of his first acts was to promote Sherman to full general in command of the Army; then he elevated Sheridan to lieutenant general. Meade, two months Sheridan's senior as a major general, keenly felt Grant's snub. Sherman reassigned the ailing general to Philadelphia, allowing Meade to stay home with his family as he attended to light duties. His old 1862 wound seemed to attract bouts of pneumonia. The general was stricken with one such attack on October 31, 1872, which led to his death on November 6. A grief-stricken city turned out for the November 11 funeral. Pallbearers included Generals Sheridan, Humphreys, Parke, and Wright, together with four Navy admirals. President Grant and General Sherman both attended the proceedings as well. Veterans of the Pennsylvania Reserves marched en masse, carrying their old, war-torn battle flags, borrowed for the occasion from Harrisburg. Old Baldy followed along in the procession, which began at St. Mark's Episcopal

Church, and ended up at the Schuylkill River. There, the casket was loaded onto a barge for a brief voyage upstream to Laurel Hill Cemetery, where the general's remains were laid to rest in the Sergeant family plot. His tombstone reads as follows:

> George Gordon Meade
> Major General U. S. Army
> Born at Cadiz, Spain
> Dec. 31, 1815
> Died at Philadelphia
> Nov. 6, 1872
> He did his work bravely
> and is at rest

Meade's tombstone inscription aptly sums up the general's career. He was a competent and solid commander who at times went against conventional wisdom and pressure and refused to sacrifice troops when battlefield conditions were adverse to success. His conduct in the battles in which he fought showed that Meade was a cautious but reliable commander. His training and subsequent career as an engineer meant that he approached problems in a methodical manner. General Lee, on hearing that Meade had superseded Hooker in command of the Army of the Potomac, is reported to have said: "General Meade will commit no blunder in my front, and if I make one he will make haste to take advantage of it."[2]

Although competent, Meade was also typical of his era, a soldier who followed orders, sometimes got lucky, and always maintained the usual military caution that characterized commanders during the war. While in command of the Army of the Potomac, Meade's focus was on strategy that dealt with Lee's army in particular, the defense of Washington, and the more distant view of capturing Richmond. While Meade reversed the Army of the Potomac's string of defeats, he was clearly not the man to win the Civil War. But he was also not the man who would lose the war either.

It is unfortunate, as his chief of staff, Alexander Webb, said, that Meade was honest to a fault and had to deal with "unworthy generals" such as Dan Sickles. These men, as well as others who came in contact with Meade, some of them experiencing his legendary temper, left unflattering impressions of the general that have been repeated through the years by uncritical writers. As a result, Meade has never received the credit due to him. Even the victory at Gettysburg, the pinnacle of Meade's military career, was besmirched by a group of vindictive officers who sought to undercut his success. A number of the general's peers also sought to embellish their own careers at Meade's expense. But in recent years, a more balanced picture of Meade has begun to emerge, in spite of the negative literature relied upon by previous historians. Meade can now rest.

Notes

Preface
  1. Horace Porter, *Campaigning with Grant* (New York: The Century Company, 1897), 247.
  2. George Meade, *The Life and Letters of George Gordon Meade* (1913; reprint, Baltimore: Butternut & Blue, 1994), 2:271.

Chapter 1
  1. Meade, *Life and Letters*, 1:38.
  2. Meade, *Life and Letters* 1:139.

Chapter 2
  1. Meade, *Life and Letters*, 2:218.
  2. Meade, *Life and Letters*, 1:220.
  3. Meade, *Life and Letters*, 1:223.
  4. Meade, *Life and Letters*, 1:231.

Chapter 3
  1. Meade, *Life and Letters*, 1:303–4.
  2. Meade, *Life and Letters*, 1:305.
  3. Meade, *Life and Letters*, 1:308.

Chapter 4
  1. Meade, *Life and Letters*, 1:337.
  2. Osmund R. H. Thomson and William H. Rauch, *History of the "Bucktails," Kane Rifle Regiment of the Pennsylvania Reserve Corps (13th Pennsylvania Reserves 42nd of the Line)* (1906; reprint, Dayton, Ohio: Morningside House, 1988), 236.

3. Freeman Cleaves, *Meade of Gettysburg* (Norman: University of Oklahoma Press, 1960; reprint, Dayton, Ohio: Morningside Bookshop, 1980), 110.

4. Meade, *Life and Letters*, 1:375.

5. Meade, *Life and Letters*, 1:373.

6. United States War Department, *The War of the Rebellion: A Compilation of the Official Records of the Union and Confederate Armies*, 70 volumes, 128 parts (Washington, D.C.: Government Printing Office, 1880–1901), series 1, vol. 27, pt. 1, 61.

7. Meade, *Life and Letters*, 2:4.

Chapter 5

1. U.S. War Department, *Official Records*, vol. 27, pt. 1, 366.

2. Richard A. Sauers, "'Rarely Has More Skill, Vigor, or Wisdom Been Shown': George G. Meade on July 3 at Gettysburg," in *Three Days at Gettysburg: Essays on Confederate and Union Leadership at Gettysburg*, ed. Gary W. Gallagher (Kent, Ohio: Kent State University Press, 1999), 242.

Chapter 6

1. Meade, *Life and Letters*, 2:308.

2. U.S. War Department, *Official Records*, vol. 27, pt. 1, 700.

3. U.S. War Department, *Official Records*, vol. 27, pt. 1, 93.

4. Meade, *Life and Letters*, 2:138.

5. U.S. War Department, *Official Records*, vol. 29, pt. 2, 346.

6. Meade, *Life and Letters*, 2:158.

7. Meade, *Life and Letters*, 2:169.

8. Meade, *Life and Letters*, 2:178.

Chapter 7

1. Cleaves, *Meade of Gettysburg*, 232.

2. George R. Agassiz, ed., *Meade's Headquarters 1863–1865: Letters of Colonel Theodore Lyman from The Wilderness to Appomattox* (Boston: Atlantic Monthly Press, 1922), 87.

3. Charles A. Dana, *Recollections of the Civil War* (New York: Collier Books, 1963), 171–72.

4. Meade, *Life and Letters*, 2:196.

5. Meade, *Life and Letters*, 2:197–8.

6. Agassiz, *Meade's Headquarters*, 91.

7. Agassiz, *Meade's Headquarters*, 126.

8. Meade, *Life and Letters*, 2:201.

9. Meade, *Life and Letters*, 2:341.

10. Meade, *Life and Letters*, 2:202.

11. John Gibbon, *Personal Recollections of the Civil War* (1928; reprint, Dayton, Ohio: Morningside Bookshop, 1978, 1994), 240.

Chapter 8

1. Cleaves, *Meade at Gettysburg*, 263.

2. Porter, *Campaigning with Grant*, 209.

3. Adam Badeau, *Military History of Ulysses S. Grant, from April 1861 to April 1865*. 3 vols. (New York: D. Appleton, 1868–81), 3:385.

4. Quotes are from the Meade letter and comments in John Y. Simon, ed., *The Papers of Ulysses S. Grant*, 24 volumes to date (Carbondale: University of Illinois Press, 1967–), 11:104–5. A copy is also in the Meade Papers, Historical Society of Pennsylvania.

5. Meade, *Life and Letters*, 2:218–19, 221.

Chapter 9

1. Agassiz, *Meade's Headquarters*, 351.

2. Cleaves, *Meade at Gettysburg*, 332.

3. Agassiz, *Meade's Headquarters*, 360.

4. Meade, *Life and Letters*, 2:271.

5. *Philadelphia Inquirer*, July 5, 1866. Meade's speech was covered in other Philadelphia newspapers as well.

Chapter 10

1. Quoted in Kenneth W. Munden and Henry P. Beers, *Guide to Federal Archives Relating to the Civil War* (Washington, D.C.: Government Printing Office, 1962), 415.

2. Edwin B. Coddington, *The Gettysburg Campaign: A Study in Command* (New York: Charles Scribner's Sons, 1968; reprint, Dayton, Ohio: Press of Morningside, 1979), 196, quoting from David Donald, ed., *A Rebel's Recollections* (Bloomington: Indiana University Press, 1959), 130.

Bibliography

1. Meade, *Life and Letters*, 2:184.

Bibliographic Note

Previous scholarship on Meade has been limited when compared to other Union generals who held army command. In 1864, the Philadelphia firm of T. B. Peterson & Brothers printed a pamphlet titled "Life and Public Services of Major General Meade (George Gordon Meade), the Hero of Gettysburg and Commander of the Army of the Potomac," an anonymous brief synopsis of the general's history thus far. After seeing a copy of this pamphlet, Meade wrote to his wife that "I had no idea my services would take up so much printing matter. I must confess I think a little more space might be given to my services prior to the Rebellion. I always thought my services in the construction of lighthouses, and subsequently the Lake Survey, were of considerable importance."[1]

There are only three full-length biographies of the general. The first, written by nephew Richard M. Bache, was *Life of General George Gordon Meade, Commander of the Army of the Potomac* (Philadelphia: Henry T. Coates, 1897; rev. ed., Philadelphia: John C. Winston, 1906). The second appeared in 1901 as part of Appleton's "Great Commanders" series, and was written by fellow Pennsylvanian Isaac R. Pennypacker, *General Meade* (New York: D. Appleton and Company, 1901). The best biography thus far was by amateur historian Freeman Cleaves, *Meade of Gettysburg* (Norman: University of Oklahoma Press, 1960; reprint, Dayton, Ohio: Morningside Bookshop, 1980). Although much better than the previous two biographies, Cleaves made a number of factual errors; his book would also have been better with more research in other archival collections.

The starting point for any research on Meade is the large collection of Meade papers in the Historical Society of Pennsylvania. Included in this collection are the papers of Col. George Meade, his father's staunch defender after the general's death in 1872. The colonel's son, also named George, published the two-volume *The Life and Letters of George Gordon Meade* (1913; reprint, Baltimore: Butternut & Blue, 1994), which includes the general's letters to his wife, Margaret, during the Civil War. The Gettysburg section of *Life and Letters* was published separately, with some minor alterations, as *With Meade at Gettysburg* (Philadelphia: John C. Winston Company, 1930).

The papers of several of Meade's contemporaries also provide much source material on the general. Especially important are the papers of Andrew A. Humphreys in the Historical Society of Pennsylvania and those of Alexander S. Webb at Yale University. The Historical Society of Pennsylvania also contains the Civil War letters of Maj. James C. Biddle, one of Meade's prominent staff officers. John Gibbon's wartime letters are also in the Historical Society of Pennsylvania.

Published recollections of Meade's contemporaries shed some light on his role during the Civil War. These include John Gibbon, *Personal Recollections of the Civil War* (1928; reprint, Dayton, Ohio: Press of Morningside Bookshop, 1978, 1994); Charles A. Dana, *Recollections of the Civil War* (New York: Collier Books, 1963); George R. Agassiz, ed., *Meade's Headquarters 1863–1865: Letters of Colonel Theodore Lyman from The Wilderness to Appomattox* (Boston: Atlantic Monthly Press, 1922); Horace Porter, *Campaigning with Grant* (New York: The Century Company, 1897); David S. Sparks, ed., *Inside Lincoln's Army: The Diary of Marsena Rudolph Patrick, Provost Marshal General, Army of the Potomac* (New York: Thomas Yoseloff, 1964); and Benjamin P. Thomas, ed., *Three Years with Grant, as Recalled by War Correspondent Sylvanus Cadwallader* (New York: Alfred A. Knopf, 1955).

The more important secondary studies include Richard A. Sauers, *Gettysburg: The Meade-Sickles Controversy* (Dulles, Virginia: Brassey's, 2003); Edwin B. Coddington, "The Strange

Reputation of George G. Meade: A Lesson in Historiography," *The Historian* 23 (1962): 145–66; Arthur V. Grant Jr., "Unity of Command: The Command Relationship between Generals Grant and Meade in the Campaigns of 1864–1865" (master's thesis, Rice University, 1974); Richard A. Sauers, "'Rarely Has More Skill, Vigor, or Wisdom Been Shown': George G. Meade on July 3 at Gettysburg," in *Three Days at Gettysburg: Essays on Confederate and Union Leadership at Gettysburg,* ed. Gary W. Gallagher (Kent, Ohio: Kent State University Press, 1999), 231–44; Stephen W. Sears, "Meade Takes Command," *North & South* 5 (September 2002): 12–20; Bruce Tap, "'Bad Faith Somewhere': George Gordon Meade and the Committee on the Conduct of the War," *North & South* 2 (August 1999): 74–81; and Frank J. Williams, "'We Had Only to Stretch Forth Our Hands': Abraham Lincoln and George Gordon Meade," *North & South* 2 (August 1999): 66–72.

Index

About the Author

A native of Lewisburg, Pennsylvania, Richard A. Sauers received his B.A. in history from Susquehanna University, and his M.A. and Ph.D. in history from Pennsylvania State University. Sauers is the author of more than twenty books, including *The Gettysburg Campaign* bibliography (1982), the highly acclaimed two-volume *Advance the Colors! Pennsylvania Civil War Battle Flags* (1987–1991), *A Succession of Honorable Victories: The Burnside Expedition in North Carolina* (1996), *Pennsylvania in the Spanish-American War: A Commemorative Look Back* (1998), *How to Do Civil War Research* (2000), *Ricketts' Battery* (2001), and *Gettysburg: The Meade-Sickles Controversy* (2003). Other writings include fifteen journal articles, more than ninety encyclopedia articles, nine introductions, and three hundred book reviews.

MILITARY PROFILES
AVAILABLE

Farragut: America's First Admiral
Robert J. Scneller Jr.
Drake: For God, Queen, and Plunder
Wade G. Dudley
Santa Anna: A Curse Upon Mexico
Robert L. Scheina
Eisenhower: Soldier-Statesman of the American Century
Douglas Kinnard
Semmes: Rebel Raider
John M. Taylor
Doolittle: Aerospace Visionary
Dik Alan Daso
Foch: Supreme Allied Commander in the Great War
Michael S. Neiberg
Villa: Soldier of the Mexican Revolution
Robert L. Scheina
Cushing: Civil War SEAL
Robert J. Schneller Jr.
Alexander the Great: Invincible King of Macedonia
Peter G. Tsouras
Rickover: Father of the Nuclear Navy
Thomas B. Allen and Norman Polmar
Forrest: The Confederacy's Relentless Warrior
Robert M. Browning Jr.
Meade: Victor of Gettysburg
Richard A. Sauers

MILITARY PROFILES
FORTHCOMING

Halsey
Robert J. Cressman

Tirpitz
Michael Epkenhans

Petain
Robert B. Bruce

Winfield Scott
Samuel Watson

Benedict Arnold
Mark Hayes